Plato's *Phaedrus*

The Focus Philosophical Library

Plato's *Phaedrus*

A translation with notes, glossary, appendices,
Interpretive Essay and Introduction

Stephen Scully

Albert Keith Whitaker
Series Editor

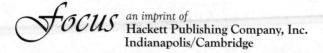

an imprint of
Hackett Publishing Company, Inc.
Indianapolis/Cambridge

Cover: Winged Eros mounting a chariot drawn by two horses. Athenian Red Figure, circa 420 BCE. Oenochoe. National Museum of Athens 1736 (CC1307). Courtesy National Archaelogical Museum, Athens/Photo: Archaelogical Receipts Fund (TAP Service).

ISBN-13: 978-0-941051-54-5

Previously published by Focus Publishing / R. Pullins Company

focus an imprint of
Hackett Publishing Company, Inc.
P.O. Box 44937
Indianapolis, Indiana 46244-0937

www.hackettpublishing.com

19 18 17 16 15   6 7 8 9 10

CONTENTS

INTRODUCTION

The *Phaedrus* is Plato's least political dialogue. Its central themes—rhetoric, love, the soul—recur throughout Plato's writings, but philosophically, poetically, and topographically, the *Phaedrus* is a world apart. Socrates pays lip-service in this dialogue to the public role of rhetoric in the political assemblies and the law-courts, but he defines the art of rhetoric as "soul-leading" in one-on-one exchange, the only true occasion for philosophy. Phaedrus, the single other person in the dialogue, is bewildered when he first hears this definition. The conception of love is also completely stripped of any political relevance. This sets the *Phaedrus* far apart from both the *Symposium* and *Republic*, with which it otherwise has much in common. In the *Symposium*, the competing pulls between earthly and heavenly love, between rewards of the flesh and of the spirit, are dramatized in the figure of Alcibiades, at a cross-roads in his life between following a philosophical path or continuing in his promising political career. The storm clouds of the disastrous Sicilian expedition and of the condemnation of Alcibiades in the law courts which will break over Athens a few months after the fictional setting of the *Symposium* suggest how important Alcibiades' inner struggle will be for the welfare of the city. Questions about love no less permeate the *Republic*'s search for an ideal political regime. Not so in the *Phaedrus*. Like the views of rhetoric, views of love in this dialogue are far removed from the political arena.

In other Platonic dialogues, moderation is a cardinal virtue, recognized for its key role in enabling a soul or a state to attain harmony within itself. In the *Phaedrus* as well, moderation is honored for its role in taming monstrous appetite and leading the soul towards a vision of heavenly Beauty, but in the climactic paragraph of his second speech Socrates chastises *mortal* moderation for its miserly, economizing, and slavish nature, saying that a soul led by (mortal) moderation alone and not driven wild by love will be condemned to roam for 9,000 years in mindless fashion around the earth, and beneath it. A divine madness, infused with erotic passion, must seized the soul if it ever hopes to recall its former life in the heavens among the gods. This is an ecstatic vision, cut free in significant ways from Plato's normal political preoccupations.

The reason for this anomaly is not hard to find. Late in the morning on a blistering hot summer day, Socrates saw his younger friend, barefoot, headed toward the city gate. Asked where he is headed, Phaedrus says that he is going to the country to practice a brilliant speech which he heard Lysias deliver the day before. This is enough to seduce Socrates to go outside Athens in the hope that Phaedrus' speech-making will cure him of his passion for speeches. On the way out, Socrates sees something bulging under Phaedrus' cloak and surmises, correctly, that it must be the papyrus roll of Lysias' *written* text. Socrates now insists that Phaedrus find a suitable place to read this to him.

Phaedrus leads Socrates to a grove, shaded by a tall plane tree, on the far side of the river Ilissos. It turns out to be a fortuitous choice. A moderate breeze blows through the grove; in addition to the shade of the plane tree, there is a tall willow shrub in full bloom, diffusing throughout the grove a pleasant perfume. The men's feet are cooled by a spring below, and overhead a chorus of cicadas sing, causing the breeze to reverberate with their high-pitched song. Underfoot are soft grasses. It also happens that the grove is sacred, the haunt of nymphs and the river god Achelous, as the statues there testify, and, as we learn later, it is sacred to Pan ("All").[1]

This grove prefigures many important retreats in later ancient literature. Its features are replicated in pastoral poetry, for example in Theocritus' *Idylls* and in Vergil's *Eclogues*. Events in the *Phaedrus* also shape conventional pastoral themes: poets in the company of nymphs, the concern for art and song-making, talk of boy-love, contests between speakers, often with a judge mediating. Many features of the grove (without the statues of the gods) will also re-appear in the form of the Epicurean garden, the place of retreat and philosophical tranquility where true fellowship and discourse can occur away from the distractions of city-life (cf. Lucretius, *De Rerum Natura* II.29-33). With the re-introduction of the *Phaedrus* to the west in the 1480s, western literature will again be touched by the power of such a place to alter the imagination. To quote Theseus from *A Midsummer Night's Dream* (V.i): "The poet's eye, in a fine frenzy rolling,/ Doth glance from heaven to earth, from earth to heaven;/ And as imagination bodies forth/ The forms of things unknown, the poet's pen/ Turns them to shapes, and gives to airy nothing/ A local habitation and a name." [2]

---

[1]   See Glosssary under *Grove*.
[2]   See Appendix E.

The grove has no less an effect upon Socrates. When he has first arrived, Socrates says in a famous passage: "Country places and trees do not wish to teach me anything, but human beings in the city do." In thinking this, Socrates is following the maxim inscribed on Apollo's temple at Delphi, "know thyself," which the city philosopher interprets in the sense that human nature differs from nature's nature. But Socrates still has much to learn about the human. Later in the dialogue, he will compare himself to Odysseus passing by the Sirens unscathed; the journey he is about to go on is in many ways more far-flung than Odysseus' from Troy to Ithaca.

Although Phaedrus is in the lead and comments that Socrates looks totally out of place and appears *never* to have left Athens, by some peculiar turn Socrates knows more about where they are than Phaedrus does, and he is clearly the one who responds to the charms of this "all-beautiful (*pan-kalos*) place." In short order he will be "nymph-possessed" and sense that he "has a god within." The language of divine possession runs throughout the first half of the *Phaedrus*; some of the early references may be said in jest or with a sense of Socratic irony but they should not be dismissed out of hand. In his second speech Socrates will praise divine madness as a gift (manifest in four forms) and recognize "en-thusiasm," literally "having the god within" as necessary for soul-travel. If he were not in this place it is doubtful whether Socrates could describe the unencumbered soul's dance with the gods in heaven or the realm of Being beyond heaven which no poet here on earth has ever described before.[3]

A word about the structure of the *Phaedrus*. After Socrates and Phaedrus come to the grove, the dialogue consists of three speeches on love (at least, formally), followed by a long discourse on the art of rhetoric. There is no more difficult task in reading the *Phaedrus* than to determine finally what holds it together: rhetoric, love, the soul, the idea of Beauty, philosophy. It is a question that has been asked since antiquity. The problem is all the more surprising because in the discussion of rhetoric Socrates says that any good composition, like a living creature, should have a head, guiding it. So, what is the head of the *Phaedrus*?[4]

The first speech, by Lysias, is read out loud, on the clever, if morally repugnant, theme that the beloved should grant his favors to a non-lover rather than to a lover. Phaedrus is greatly impressed by it, an epideictic show piece designed to advertise Lysias' rhetorical prowess. But far from being cured by hearing it, Socrates feels that he can do better, influenced in this belief in part by something he has heard from ancient writers (he suspects from the poets Sappho and Anacreon) and in part by Dionysos, by the gods of the grove, and by Phaedrus himself. This leads to Socrates'

---

[3] See "Interpretative Essay," pages 94-5 and Glossary under *Divine possession*.
[4] For an extended discussion of the unity of the *Phaedrus*, see the Interpretative Essay.

first speech which, Phaedrus stipulates, must be on the same topic as Lysias' speech. But it also differs: Lysias is a *poietes* while Socrates calls himself an *idiotes*; Lysias' speech was written, Socrates' will be impromptu.[5] Socrates feels shame as he delivers his speech, his head hidden under his cloak the whole time he speaks. He concludes abruptly and never does praise the virtue of a non-lover; his challenge over, he is eager to cross the river and head back to Athens when his private spirit (or daemon) says "no." As is the custom of this daemon, no explanation is offered, but Socrates comes to realize (with the help of some lines from the poet Ibycus) that he has offended Eros, the god of Love, who must now be appeased. Thus begins Socrates' visionary second speech, called a palinode after the famous palinode by Stesichorus when the poet took back what he said in his first poem about Helen going to Troy. In doing so, Stesichorus, unlike Homer, regained his eyesight. Socrates hopes to make amends with Eros before he is similarly maimed.

As was true of Lysias, Socrates in his first speech is as interested in rhetoric as he is in his subject matter. But in the second speech (also impromptu), talk of rhetoric vanishes, as if what Socrates has to say pushes aside commentary on how he should be saying it. In the palinode, Socrates will distinguish between two kinds of madness, one the product of human illness, the other a divine gift, "the greatest of all good things" to come to humankind. He divides divine madness into four kinds: mantic, from Apollo; initiation into the mysteries ascribed to Dionysos; poetic madness from the Muses; erotic, the fourth and best, from Aphrodite and Eros. The speech is clearly ecstatic, revealing what "no poet has done before": the winged soul (in the form of a charioteer driving a pair of horses, one white, the other black), dancing with the gods in the heavens and looking with them from the rim of heaven to the immortal Forms beyond heaven. In time, Socrates reports, the soul will lose her wings and fall to earth. Only a divinely-inspired erotic madness (not the "unnatural" kind leading to procreation) can cause those heavenly wings to re-sprout, enabling ascent after the soul is freed from the mortal body.[6]

A discussion on the art of rhetoric follows in the second half of the dialogue, Phaedrus saying next to nothing about the content of the palinode. Accordingly, the *Phaedrus* is often divided into two halves: speeches in the first half, the rather somber discussion of art in the second. Or, one might consider dividing the dialogue into thirds: the first and third parts about speech-making, framing a vision of love and the immortal soul in the middle. It is during the discussion of rhetoric that Socrates proposes a definition of rhetoric as soul-guiding which befuddles Phaedrus initially.

---

[5]   See Glossary under *Unskilled speaker* and the Interpretative Essay, pages 91-4.
[6]   See the Interpretative Essay, pages 80-2.

A word about boy-love in the *Phaedrus*. It refers to the ancient Greek custom of an older man *(erastes*, or lover) being sexually aroused by a "beloved" (an *eromenos)*, also called a "boy" *(pais)* or "darling" *(paidika)*. As seen in archaic poetry, Eros (Love) is an illness which seizes, melts, burns, freezes, whips, pierces body and soul, "shaking the heart like a wind rushing down upon a tree," to quote from the seventh-century poet Sappho (fr. 47). Ancient Greek pederasty ("love of a boy") is often equated with our modern term "homosexuality," though the two forms of love are distinct in a number of crucial ways. According to the standard modern interpretation, the ancient Greek relationship between lover and beloved was far from symmetrical or reciprocal. In this model, an older man (the *erastes)*, driven by *eros* (sexual passion), pursues a sexually passive boy (the *eromenos*) who seeks *philia* (friendship) from the relationship. The lover's apparent advantage from age, experience, and social station, however, is more than offset by the boy's beauty which drives the man into a frenzy, and by the boy's power to choose between various suitors. In return for the lover's attention, the beloved is expected to "gratify" *(charizesthai)* the lover sexually, which takes the form of the man rubbing his penis between the boy's thighs (what is known as the intercrural position). In theory, penetration in any form is scorned. The beloved would be ostracized if he sought sexual pleasure for himself. His reward is, minimally, material benefit and, ideally, affection and social advancement into adult (male) life. Much of the talk about love in the *Phaedrus* conforms to this asymmetrical model. From this perspective, Lysias' argument that a boy should grant favors to a non-lover appears to offer a radical, and witty, departure from convention, but Socrates' vision in the palinode of erotic reciprocity between man and boy would be a much deeper challenge to Greek same-sex eroticism. Recent studies, however, have shown that in Athens by 400 BCE sexual mores were changing: love between men of the same age (usually adolescents and young adults) was increasingly common, and reciprocal sexual gratification no longer socially scorned. Socrates' reiteration of a popular saying, "the young delight in the young" (240c), may indeed reflect these new mores. In short, we may conclude that sexual conventions and the respective ages of the *erastes* and the *eromenos* were in flux at the time Plato was writing the *Phaedrus*. While the *erastes* may typically have been an adult and married, he could be no more than an aging adolescent, and the *eromenos*, in theory a beardless boy, in practice could be as old as thirty or even thirty-five, in which case he might have shaved in an effort to retain his "boyish" looks.[7]

---

[7]   For the conventional view, see Kenneth Dover, *Greek Homosexuality* (London, 1978) and David Halperin, "Homosexuality" in *The Oxford Classical Dictionary* 3rd ed. (Oxford, 1996) 720-23. For the necessary modifications of this view, see T. K. Hubbard (ed.), *Homosexuality in Greece and Rome: A Sourcebook of Basic Documents* (Berkeley, 2003).

Even given this flexibility of conventions, the sexual relations between the various players in the *Phaedrus* are confusing, no doubt deliberately so. It is easy to imagine Lysias' speech as an effort to seduce Phaedrus or anyone else who might happen to hear or read him. In this context, the renowned rhetorician Lysias would be the (non)-*erastes* and Phaedrus the *eromenos*. But on two occasions, Lysias is said to be Phaedrus' "darling," as the up-and-coming rhetorician Isocrates is called Socrates' "darling." If we fix the dramatic date of the *Phaedrus* at 410 BCE,[8] the historical Socrates would be 59 and his "darling" Isocrates 26, while Phaedurs would be in his late thirties and his "darling" Lysias 48, an absurd idea.[9] But histori-cal verisimilitude should not be pushed too strenuously. The characters of

---

[8]   Lysias was out of Athens from 415 to 412/411 BCE, making the possible dramatic dates of the *Phaedrus* either 418-416 or 411-404. Both positions have been forcefully argued. The earlier date links the dialogue more closely in dramatic time to Plato's *Symposium*, doubly placed in 415 and 400; the later date overlaps with the dramatic date for Plato's *Republic*. As indicated in the notes to this translation, quite a few passages in the *Phaedrus* recall passages from a number of other Platonic dialogues, but particularly from either the *Symposium* or the *Republic*. In one instance Phaedrus seems to be jokingly referring to the *Republic* (cf. 276e).

[9]   Socrates' dates are 469-399 BCE; he is an Athenian. Lysias' dates are (circa) 459-380 BCE. He is a resident "metic" in Athens, a technical term for a for-eigner with many legal rights. He lived in Athens until his father Kephalos died, when he moved to Thurii in southern Italy in 415 before coming back to Athens in 412-411. He and his brother Polemarkhos were arrested by the Thirty Tyrants in 403; Polemarkhos was killed and Lysias barely escaped. He returned with the democratic forces later that year. Plato's *Republic* takes place in Kephalos' house in Piraeus, Athens' port. Phaedrus was an Athe-nian born circa 450 BCE; he also appears in Plato's *Protagoras* and *Sympo-sium*. Isocrates (an Athenian born in 436) is only mentioned once at the end of the dialogue but some consider him to be the true object of Plato's at-tack against conventional rhetoric. He lived to the age of 98, dying in 338 BCE. He considered himself a philosopher whose teaching was embodied in a principle of education based on rhetorical training. Like Socrates in this dialogue, he claimed that he was an *idiotes*, by which he meant something quite different from Socrates (see note 19 and Glossary under *Unskilled speaker*). Plato, also an Athenian, is Isocrates' younger contemporary and rival; he is born circa 429 and dies in 347. Another rhetorician, Alkidamas, is not named in the dialogue but a number of phrases in the *Phaedrus* are also found in his tract against rhetoricians who, like Isocrates, relied on writing rather than extemporaneous composition. It is not possible to determine whether the *Phaedrus* or Alkidamas' treatise against writers is earlier. Alkidamas was born in Elaia in Aiolis in Asia Minor and came to Athens sometime in the fourth century to teach rhetoric. (For an excerpt of Alkidamas' treatise on written and extemporaneous speeches, see Appendix D).

the *Phaedrus*, like its grove, are elements in a drama that has only an approxiamte relation to literal reality.[10]

Within the context of the dialogue, it seems natural to see Socrates as trying to seduce Phaedrus away from Lysias. The exchanges between Socrates and Phaedrus can be sexually playful; once Socrates even addresses Phaedrus as "my boy" (267c). But how serious is this play? Physical intimacy and philosophy need not be incompatible, as the Zeus/Ganymede model shows (255a-c). But how close a model is Ganymede for Phaedrus?[11] Both of Socrates' speeches are addressed to a "beautiful (darling) boy," the same boy addressed in Lysias' speech. Is Socrates *also* playfully addressing his companion? Phaedrus clearly wants to think that he is. Just before the palinode when Socrates asks "Where is the boy with whom I was just speaking?," Phaedrus responds: "That boy's right here, always by your side whenever you wish" (243e).

If Socrates is trying to seduce Phaedrus, he, unlike Lysias, is not interested in a physical conquest. Socrates concludes the palinode with a prayer to Eros that Phaedrus who is "going in two directions" be turned toward a love of philosophy. In a narrow sense, Phaedrus is torn between Lysias' and Socrates' speeches; more broadly, he must decide between sophistic and philosophical rhetoric, that is, between style and form on the one hand and truth and pursuit of wisdom on the other. Socrates prays to turn Phaedrus' love for surface beauty towards a love of wisdom and true Beauty. In thinking about the unity of the *Phaedrus*, one might conjecture that its "head" lies here: the uniting theme of soul-turning, whether through divinely-inspire love or the philosophically trained rhetorician guiding souls. By the end of the dialogue, Phaedrus will embrace Socrates' peculiar definition of rhetoric and his claims that true rhetoric must serve the needs of philosophy. The "boy's" acceptance of these stipulations suggests that the philosopher has succeeded, at least temporarily, in taming the more undisciplined aspects of Phaedrus' tastes and in re-orienting his soul.

---

[10]   So Cicero also argued; cf. *De Oratore* 1.7.28.

[11]   One's point of view affects translation. After his palinode, Socrates calls upon "noble creatures"—arguments—to persuade *kallipaida...Phaidron*, that unless he learns to love wisdom he will never become a competent speaker. Literally *kallipaida* means "beautiful boy" (261a); some scholars argue that the word links this new turn in the dialogue to Socrates' speech on divine erotic madness just concluded, as there he called his addressee "my beautiful (darling) boy" (*o pai kale*, 243e; cf. 267c). But others who downplay the attraction between the two interlocutors tend to follow an ancient commentator who claimed that *kallipaida* means "a father of beautiful offspring," i.e. that Phaedrus is a begetter of speeches, as Socrates implies at 242a-b. I translate *kallipaida* "beautiful boy," by far the more likely meaning of the word.

TRANSLATOR'S NOTE

The range in tone, style, and vocabulary in the *Phaedrus* is enormous. My first effort as translator is to capture in English the lively spirit of exchange and discovery in the conversation and the great rhetorical variety from one speech to the next, while still adhering as closely as possible to the Greek. At the level of the sentence, I try to replicate in English what I see as the points of emphasis in the Greek. This can require a rearrangement of clauses or converting a participle to a main verb, or vice versa. Greek has small parts of speech called "particles" which serve as sentence "dividers" and show how a sentence is to be read in the context of what comes before it. A good deal of effort is spent in trying to convey these colorings in English. In the speeches, I also try to identify the logical units of thought, again often marked by "particles." At times, my paragraph breaks differ from those found in Burnet's Oxford text of 1901 which I followed for the most part.

Most of the Greek names are rendered in their more familiar Latinate forms: so Phaedrus instead of Phaidros, Alcibiades instead of Alkibiades, Achelous instead of Akheloos, for example. For less familiar names, like Kephalos, Akoumenos, Oreithuia, and Pharmakeia, I have retained the Greek spellings.

As mentioned in Appendix E, Marsilio Ficino translated the complete works of Plato into Latin in 1484 (Florence; 2nd edition published in Venice in 1491). The first printed edition of Plato's works in Greek was published by the Aldine press in Venice in 1513, with the assistance of the great Greek scholar Marcus Musurus. In 1534 at Basle, Valder, with the aid of Simon Grynaeus, published an edition of Plato's works along with Proclus' commentary. In 1578 at Paris, Henricus Stephanus (Henri Estienne, or Henry Stephens), aided by Johannes Serranus (Jean de Serae) published in three folio volumes a grand edition of Plato's works which were dedicated to

Queen Elizabeth, King James VI of Scotland, and the Consuls of the Republic of Berne, respectively. The pages of the folio were subdivided into five parts ([a], b, c, d, e) and these pages and letterings, printed in the margins of modern editions, have become the standard basis of reference for Plato's corpus.

It has been a most enjoyable experience to translate this dialogue, largely thanks to my students in a *Phaedrus* seminar, and it is to them that I wish to dedicate this translation: Collomia Charles, Darcie Hutchison, Stuart Koonce, Theodore Korzukhin, Melissa Mitchell, Jonathan Schwiebert, Michael Skor, and Franco Trivigno.

I also owe a great debt of thanks to Frank Nisetich, Harry Thomas, Jonathon Aaron, Michael Keating and Kathleen Lancaster, and to my wife, Rosanna Warren, mystery and book.

OUTLINE

PLATO'S *PHAEDRUS*

Socrates: My dear Phaedrus, where have you been? And where are you going? 227a

Phaedrus: I've been with Lysias, Kephalos' son,[1] Socrates, and now I'm going for a walk outside the city walls. I've been with him a long time, since dawn in fact. Now I'm headed for the country, following the advice of our friend, Akoumenos,[2] who says it's more refreshing to walk there than in our city's covered colonnades.[3]

b

---

[1] Kephalos was what the Athenians called a *metic*, a resident alien with special legal rights. He was extremely wealthy with a fortune made from selling arms. He lived in Piraeus, Athens' port, where he also had his arms factory, and it was at his home that the *Republic* takes place. Lysias' brother, Polemarchos, is mentioned at 257c for being more philosophical than Lysias. Polemarchos has a speaking part in the *Republic* and was killed by the Thirty in 404 BCE for his money.

[2] Akoumenos is a doctor, and father (or older relative) of Eruximachos, also a doctor, Phaedrus' lover, and a speaker in Plato's *Symposium*. All three are sympathetic to the new sophistic movement. References to doctors and medical terminology permeate the dialogue, in the discussion both of love and of rhetoric. Like most ancient Greeks, Lysias considered love a sickness (231d), a view which Socrates shares in his first speech but challenges in his second speech when he says that the love of beauty is "the only doctor for the soul's greatest labors and pains" (252b). At the end of the dialogue, the art of medicine is compared to the art of rhetoric, one affecting the body, the other the soul (270b-d). The *Phaedrus* also raises the question of whether a practitioner of an art can pass his knowledge to another, either as a teacher to a pupil or a father to a son (268c-269a).

[3] Phaedrus does not say "the city's covered colonnades," but simply *dromoi* (literally: "(open) race courses"). Elsewhere Plato uses the phrase "covered

1

Socrates: Well said, my dear companion.[4] So Lysias was in town, it seems.

Phaedrus: Yes, at Epikrates' house, where Morukhos use to live, near the temple of Olympian Zeus.[5]

Socrates: How were you spending your time there? Let me guess: Lysias was feasting you with his speeches.

Phaedrus: You'll find out, if you have time to come along and listen.

Socrates: What? Don't you think I'd consider this "more important than business itself," as Pindar puts it, to hear how you and Lysias were spending your time?

c **Phaedrus:** Lead on, then.

Socrates: I will, if you speak.

Phaedrus: As a matter of fact, Socrates, our talk suited you well, because we spent our time talking about love. For Lysias has written about a beautiful boy and how he was pursued, but not by a lover, and it's just in this that Lysias was so refined. He argues that favors should be granted to one who is *not* in love with you rather than to one who is.

Socrates: What a noble man. Would that he had written that favors should be granted to someone who is poor rather than rich, and to someone who is getting on in years rather than to a younger man, and other

d such qualities which apply to me and to most of us. Now that speech would be really clever and of public use. As it is, I have already built up such a desire to hear his words that if you were to walk all the way to Megara—as far as its wall and back again (as the good doctor Herodikos prescribes), I wouldn't leave your side for all the world.[6]

---

runways" to refer to a gymnasium's colonnades and I assume that *dromoi* here is an abbreviated reference to the same place, a favorite haunt for young men to congregate.

[4] Socrates most frequently calls Phaedrus *phile*, "my friend" (11 times). For "friend," "my dear companion," and other vocative addresses to Phaedrus, and for the forms of address which Phaedrus uses in return, see the Glossary under *Vocative addresses*. Also see notes, 11, 40, 41, and 96.

[5] The comic poet Aristophanes singles out Morukhos for his lavish living. We are to assume that Lysias is also living in luxury. Images of feeding occur frequently in the first half of the *Phaedrus*, playful metaphors which become more bold in Socrates' second speech when he says that the soul feeds on or shares in the banquet of heavenly Being (247e; cf. 246e and 248b).

[6] Greek allows for a conditional construction not available in English. Socrates begins the if-clause as though it were a remote possibility, but concludes the condition in strongest possible terms ("I wouldn't leave your side").

Phaedrus: What are you saying, my Socrates, best of men? Do you think that I, a man with no speaking skills,[7] will be able to recall in a man-   **228a** ner worthy of Lysias—the most clever of our writers today—those things which he spent so much time, in leisure, arranging?[8] I'm far from that. And yet I'd rather have this ability than piles of gold.

Socrates: Phaedrus, I know you as well as I know myself; and if I don't know Phaedrus, I've forgotten myself also. But I've forgotten neither of us. I know full well that listening to Lysias' speech Phaedrus did not listen just once, but that he frequently urged him to repeat it; and Lysias was more than happy to comply. Nor was this enough for Phaedrus,   **b** but in the end he took the book and kept examining those parts which he especially coveted. Doing this since dawn he grew weary and got up from his seat to go for a walk; and now I'd say, I swear it by the dog,[9] that he knows the entire speech, unless it happens to be terribly long. Then he was headed outside the city walls to practice it. But coming upon the man who is made sick with desire just to hear speeches, Phaedrus, seeing him—merely seeing him—was delighted that he should have a fellow bacchic reveler, and then he urged Socrates to lead on. When that lover of speeches asked him to speak, Phaedrus   **c** was coy, acting as if he wasn't interested, but in the end he meant to speak, even by force, if no one wanted to listen. So, Phaedrus, ask that man to do now what he will soon do anyway.

Phaedrus: I'd better speak then as well as I can, since you don't seem about to let me go before I speak in one way or another.[10]

Socrates: That's certainly true.

Phaedrus: All right then, here's what I shall do. In reality, Socrates, I most   **d** certainly have not learnt all the words. But the general thought of Lysias' speech, and how he contrasted the lover and the non-lover— each of these things I shall go through in the order he said them, touching on the chief points, beginning with the first.

---

7   "A man with no speaking skills" translates *idiotes*; see the *Interpretative Essay* (pages 91-4) and the Glossary under *Unskilled speaker*.

8   This verb (*syntithemi*) appears four times in the space of fifteen lines at the end of the dialogue (278c-d).

9   One of Socrates' favorite oaths; it apparently refers to an Egyptian deity. See Plato's *Gorgias* 482d.

10 Socrates' compulsion reverses the scene at the beginning of the *Republic* where he wants to walk back to Athens from the port (Piraeus) but is restrained and compelled to speak.

Socrates: Only if first, my love,[11] you show me what you have in your left hand under your cloak. I'll hazard it's the actual text. And if it is, bear in mind that, as fond of you as I am,[12] I am not prepared to let you practice your speaking skills on me, not when Lysias is actually present among us. Come now, show it.

e

Phaedrus: All right, stop. You've dashed any hope, Socrates, that I had of practicing on you. But where would you like to sit down and have us read?

229a   **Socrates:** Let's turn off the path here and go along the Ilissos; then we'll sit down wherever you find a quiet spot.

Phaedrus: It's lucky, it seems, that I happen to be barefoot. You, of course, always are. So it'll be easy for us to walk with our feet in the water, and not unpleasant either, especially in this season and at this time of the day.

Socrates: Lead on then, and keep an eye out for a place to sit.

Phaedrus: Do you see that very tall plane tree?

Socrates: Yes, surely.

b   **Phaedrus:** There's shade and a moderate[13] breeze, with grass as well for sitting, or, if we prefer, we could lie down.

Socrates: Won't you lead the way?

Phaedrus: Tell me, Socrates; isn't it around here near the Ilissos where Boreas the North Wind is said to have seized Oreithuia?

Socrates: So the story goes.

Phaedrus: Is it around here, then? The waters, at least, are lovely, pure, and clear; the kind of place where girls would like to play.

---

[11] "My love" translates *philotes* (an abstract noun for the more usual concrete *phile*), a form of address found in Aristophanes; only here in Plato as a term of address. In conventional usage, *philotes* ranges in meaning from "friendhip" to "sexual intercourse." Once Socrates calls Phaedrus "my boy" (*pai*) (267c), a term lovers used for the beloved. See notes 40 and 41, and the Glossary under *Love* and *Vocative addresses*.

[12] "To be fond of" translates the verb *phileo*; for the range in meaning of this word, see the Glossary under *To Love*.

[13] Literally, a "well-measured breeze": *pneuma metrion*. The word *metron*, "measure," runs through the whole dialogue like a nerve, exploring from a variety of angles a central theme of the *Phaedrus* concerning measured speech. This will not be the only instance in the *Phaedrus* where a physical characteristic of the grove prefigures an essential theme or word in the dialogue. The grove literally embodies and makes possible the discourse of the *Phaedrus*. Socrates and Phaedrus have crossed the river and are sitting on the far side from the city (cf. 242a-c). For more on the grove, see notes 16 and 18; for *metrios*, see the Interpretative Essay (pages 92-4) and the Glossary under *Grove* and *Unskilled speaker*.

Socrates: No, but further downstream two or three stades[14] where we cross the river to the district of Agra. I think there's even an altar to Boreas in that vicinity. c

Phaedrus: I never knew exactly where it was. But tell me, Socrates, in the name of Zeus, do you really think that this mythical story is true?

Socrates: What do you mean? If, like the wise men of our day, I didn't believe in these stories, I wouldn't be so out of place. And in my wisdom, I would say that the Borean wind blew Oreithuia down from the rocks nearby while she was playing with Pharmakeia. And dying in this way, she is said to have been seized by Boreas from here—or from d the Areopagos, for there is also a story that she was seized from there. Although in some ways I find such explanations ingenious, Phaedrus, it's also true that they're the mark of a clever, hard-working, and not altogether fortunate man, if only because after these explanations he will then have to correct the mistaken beliefs about the shape of Horse Centaurs, and after that the Chimaira. Then mobs of Gorgon-like creatures, Pegasuses and other monsters will flood over him, not to men- e tion other marvelously imagined oddities. All those non-believers employing some boorish sophistication will make everything conform to probability, and they also will need a great deal of free time. But for me there's no such leisure. And, my dear friend, the reason is this: I am still not able to "know myself," as the Delphic inscription enjoins, and it seems laughable for me to think about other things when I am still ignorant about myself. So leaving those matters aside, I believe **230a** whatever people say these days about those creatures, and I don't inquire about them but about myself. For me, the question is whether I happen to be some sort of beast even more complex in form and more tumultuous than the hundred-headed Typhon, or whether I am something simpler and gentler, having a share by nature of the divine and the unTyphonic.[15] But, my dear companion, while we've been talking, haven't we reached the tree to which you were leading us?

---

14 About 1/4 mile.

15 Typhon is a monster with a hundred heads which can speak in a variety of voices at the same time. Socrates twice puns on the name Typhon, in the first instance as if the name came from the verb *typhomai*, "to be ablaze, to be caught up in a passion"; in the second instance, when Socrates questions whether he might be *atyphos*, i.e. "not deluded." In this usage, he implies that Typhon comes from *typhos*, a word for a fever which brings on a stupor, and by extension comes to mean "delusion" or "nonsense"; the negative of that *atyphos* means "humble, not arrogant, not deluded." Elsewhere Socrates says of all men: "surely some terrible, savage, and lawless form of desire is in every man, even in some of us who seem to be entirely measured (*metrios*)" (Rep. 9.572b). No mortal has an absolutely simple soul. In this dialogue, one can question who in fact has the more complex soul, closer

b   **Phaedrus:** To be sure, this is it.

    Socrates: By Hera, it's a beautiful resting-place.[16] The plane-tree is tall and has wonderfully spreading branches; and there is the lovely shade of a tall willow shrub in beautiful bloom, diffusing throughout the place a most sweet perfume. And below the plane-tree a graceful spring flows with its cooling waters,[17] as our feet bear witness. Judging from the statues and images, the spot seems sacred, a haunt of the Nymphs and
c   the river god Achelous. And, if you permit me to go on, how adorable and delightful is the gentle breeze, re-echoing with the summery, high pitch of the cicadas' chorus. And most refined of all is the grassy slope, gentle enough for lying down and resting your head most beautifully. I couldn't have hoped for a better guide, my dear Phaedrus.

    Phaedrus: And you seem, my astonishing man, to be someone most out of place.[18] As you say, you seem like a foreigner being guided around
d   rather than one from these parts, and never to have left town or traveled abroad. Indeed, I'd say, you had never ventured at all outside the city walls.

    Socrates: Pardon me, my excellent friend. I'm in love with learning. Country places and trees do not wish to teach me anything, but human

---

    in nature to Typhon's: Phaedrus or Socrates' soul. At 257b, Socrates says that Phaedrus "goes in two directions." See note 95.

[16] "Resting-place" translates *katagoge*, literally "a bringing down," an unusual word in Plato's Athens. In light of the central myth of the *Phaedrus* about the immortal soul falling down (*kata*) from heaven to earth and through love and language having the capacity to make an upward ascent (*agein ano*), the literal meaning of *katagoge* should not be ignored. In all of Plato, the term is only used here, and at 259a5 in the more usual adjectival form. In short, this grove functions as a conduit, allowing for movement up and down. *See* notes 18 and 55. In reference to the plane tree (*platanos*), one wonders whether Plato isn't punning on his own name (Platon in the moninative, Platonos in the gentive); for another possible pun on his name, see 246c. The willow shrub (*vitex agnus castus*) is found throughout the Mediterranean and is known for its fragrant violet or white flowers and for its alleged anti-aphrodisiac powers. See the Glossary under *Grove*.

[17] Socrates is paraphrasing a line from the lyric poet Sappho (fragment 2).

[18] "Most out of place" (*atopotatos*) picks up what Socrates says of himself when he says that he would not be out of place (*atopos*, 229c) if, like the wise, he did not believe in myths; he also described mythic creatures as "things out of place," translated there as "oddities" (229e). As is often the case with Socrates, Phaedrus' characterization of him as "most out of place" is steeped in paradox. Socrates is, as Phaedrus claims, indeed out of place when out of the city, but in coming to the grove Socrates is open to the divine in a new way (cf. 241e). If he were not in this divine place, it is doubtful whether Socrates could describe "the place of Being," "beyond heaven" which no *poietes* has ever described before (cf. 262d). See notes 13, 16, and 55.

beings in the city do. But you seem to have discovered a drug to entice
me into walking outside the city.[19] Just like dangling green branches
or fruit of some kind in front of a hungry animal to lead him on, so
you are likely to lead me through all of Attica or anywhere you want,   e
simply by holding words in a book in front of my nose. But now that
we have come here, I think I'll lie down. Find any position you consider comfortable and begin reading, won't you?

Phaedrus: Listen then.

You know about my affairs, and you've heard how I think
they benefit us both, when these things work out. Nor do I ex-   **231a**
pect to fail to get what I ask for just because I don't happen to be
in love with you.

When lovers lose their passion, they come to regret whatever goods they may have conferred, but these people never
have a change of heart.[20] They confer benefits according to
their means, and not by necessity, but willingly, just as they
would manage their own family interests as well as they could.

Besides, lovers keep a tally of the costs they incur and of
the benefits they confer because of love, and when they add   **b**
to the list the labor they exert, they believe that they have already paid back a sufficient gratitude to those they once loved.
But non-lovers don't blame love as an excuse for their neglect
of family matters, nor do they keep a scorecard of labors en-
dured, and they don't blame loved ones for problems with relatives. So actually when such ills are cleared out of the way
nothing is left but for non-lovers to do with zeal whatever they
think would please their partners.

---

[19] Frequently in Plato, discourse is described as a healing drug. *Pharmakos*,
"drug" (230d), is the simple noun form of *Pharmakeia* (229c), the playmate
of the girl who was killed by the North Wind near this spot. For other
uses of the word, always important in Plato, see 242e, and 274e and 275a at
the end of the *Phaedrus* in regard to writing and the god Theuth. See the
Glossary under *Drug*.

[20] Lysias begins his speech by addressing an unnamed you (in the singular) but
often references to lovers, non-lovers, and the beloved are in the impersonal,
generalizing plural. He never addresses the beloved in the vocative, giving the
impression that the speech could be said by anyone to anyone. Socrates, by
contrast, in his speeches uses the vocative address and only speaks of the loved
one in the singular (except for 252d). The ancient Greeks admired Lysias for
his clear and lucid style, but in this speech his terminology is often extremely
vague and loose: In the first line, "affairs" translates *pragmata*, a word usually
used for business or other public actions, but may on rare occasion refer to
love affairs; in stead of specifying non-lovers, in this sentence Lysias simply says
"for these people on the other hand."

c   Besides, if it is right to value lovers because they claim that they are specially fond of those they love and are ready to gratify their loved ones in word and deed, being hateful to everyone else, it is easy to see, provided lovers tell the truth, that they will value future loved ones more than those they love now. And it is clear that lovers will treat their old loves badly if the new loves so desire. And anyway, how is it plau-

d   sible[21] to hand over something so precious[22] to someone with such an affliction that no experienced person would even try to cure it: for lovers certainly agree that they are sick rather than of sound mind, and they realize that although they are thinking poorly they are powerless to do anything about it. So how can these men, once they have regained their lost senses, possibly continue to hold those beliefs which they had when they were in the grip of love?

And another thing: if you were to choose the best from the pool of lovers, your pickings would be slim; but if you were to select the one who best suits you from the general pool, your

e   range of choice would be great. So actually there is far greater hope of finding someone from this group who is worthy of your friendship.

Now, if you are worried about conventional mores and fear the scorn of people when they learn what you are doing, it is

232a   plausible that lovers (being inclined to think that they are just as worthy of emulation by others as they are by themselves) will be excited to talk about their affairs and to toot their own horn, revealing to one and all that they have not labored in vain. But non-lovers, possessing a measure of self-control, choose to do what is best rather than to follow in the foot-steps of public opinion.

Besides, everyone finds out about lovers—it's inevitable—when they see lovers following after their loves and doing any-

b   thing for them. So whenever the two are seen in conversation, everyone actually thinks that they are together, having just in-dulged in their passions or being just about to. But no one dreams of finding fault with non-lovers for their rendezvous, knowing that such talk is necessary for friendship or some other pleasure.

---

[21]   It is a hallmark of sophistic rhetoric to argue according to the plausible (*eikos*); for the general point, see 272ff. For *eikos* in Lysias' speech, see 231c (here), 231e, 232c, 233a.
[22]   i.e. chastity.

And another thing: perhaps you are afraid, thinking that it is difficult for friendships to last or that in other circumstances when a calamity arises both parties share the pain, but when you have given away freely what is most important to you,[23] you are the one who gets hurt the most. If so, it's plausible that you would fear lovers more. For all kinds of things cause them to grieve, and they think that everything is designed to hurt them. Consequently, they try to prevent those they love from meeting other people, fearful lest a wealthy person will outspend them or an educated person outsmart them. They are forever on the lookout, guarding against the possible influence of anyone who might have some advantage or other. Persuading you to become loathsome to everyone else, they leave you without friends. But if you look out after yourself and keep a cooler head than your lovers, you will end up quarrelling with them. Non-lovers, however, having acquired through virtue what they asked for, would never be jealous of your fellowship with others. Rather, they would despise those who won't associate with you on the assumption that they are being slighted and not benefiting from these encounters.[24] So actually there is far greater hope to gain friendship rather than enmity from this business.

And another thing: many lovers desire your body before they know your character or are familiar with your personal traits. So it isn't clear whether they still will wish to remain friends when they cease to desire you. But because non-lovers are friendly with each other before they exchanged favors, it is implausible that their engagement in these happy experiences would diminish their friendship; rather such things remain as tokens of things to come.

And another thing: it is fitting that you will become a better person if you are won over by me rather than by a lover. Far beyond what is best, lovers will praise whatever you say or do, in part because they fear that you will come to loathe them, in part because passion clouds their judgment. Love thinks like this: when lovers fare badly love makes them grieve over things which bring little

a problem as old as time haha

c

d

e

233a

b

---

[23] That is, when you have offered sexual favors.

[24] The lack of pronouns in this passage makes it difficult to determine who the "they" refers to, that is, whether the non-lover or the beloved is excluded from a group. It is also unclear who is thought to receive the benefit from such gatherings. Arguments have been made for both non-lover and the beloved; I am inclined to believe that the beloved is being referred to in both cases.

pain to others, and when they do well love forces them to praise even those things which are hardly worthy of pleasure. So actually it is far more fitting for loved ones to pity rather than to emulate them.

c

If I have won you over, first of all I will keep your company, not [only] looking out for immediate pleasure but also for future benefits, because I am not weakened by love but am in full possession of myself.[25] Nor do I get irate over trivial matters and only slowly build a mild anger from big problems, forgiving unintended mistakes and trying to forestall deliberate transgressions. These are proofs of a friendship which will last a long time. But if you believe that enduring friendship is not possible without erotic love, you should take to heart that we would not hold strong feelings for our sons, or fathers and mothers. Nor would we have trusted friends, who do not crop up from this sort of passion but from other kinds of pursuits.

d

Besides, if it is right to give favor to those in need, it is also entirely fitting to do a good turn to the most indigent, and not to the best people, as those who are saved from the worst ills will bestow the most thanks.

e

And another thing: even at dinner parties it is worthy not to invite friends but beggars and those in need of a meal. These are the people who will adore[26] you and follow you and come to your door and be especially pleased and express their gratitude and pray for your success.

234a

Or perhaps it is fitting to grant favors to those who are in the best position to return the favor and not to the desperately needy— in short, not only to beggars but to those worthy of your work; not to those who will enjoy you in your prime but to those who will share their own wealth with you when you have begun to age; not to those who toot their own horn, telling others when they have had their way with you, but to those who will always keep silent from a sense of decorum; not to those who are serious for a brief time, but to those who will be life-long friends; not to those who seek a pretext for enmity when their desire has dried up, but to those who will show their true merit when your bloom has ceased.

b

---

[25]   It is difficult to capture the complexity of this sentence in English. "Only" is not in the Greek, "but also" is. Lysias seems to be hinting that the non-lover *also* looks for immediate pleasure. For Socrates' severe sanction of those who desire to remain in full self-possession, see 256e-257a.

[26]   "Adore" translates *agapao* (233e3); see Glossary under *To Love*. See note 53.

Remember what I have said and take this to heart: friends chastise lovers for pursuing affairs badly, but relatives have never blamed non-lovers for planning their own business poorly because of love.

Perhaps you might ask if I advise you to grant favors to any and all non-lovers. Of course not. A lover would not demand that you have such thoughts for all lovers—for in that case he would feel that the value of each favor granted was diminished; nor would you be able to keep each favor secret. From this sort of thing, there should be no harm, only mutual benefit.

c

My words are, I trust, sufficient. But if you desire more, thinking that I have left something out, all you need do is ask.[27]

Socrates, what do you think of the speech? Isn't it extraordinary, both in its language and in other regards?

Socrates: Indeed, divinely spirited, my dear companion; naturally I'm stunned. And this I owe to you, Phaedrus, because while I was looking at you reading, you seemed lit up[28] by the speech. Thinking that you perceived such matters better than I, I followed you throughout, caught up in a bacchic frenzy with you, a divine source.[29]

d

---

[27] Lysias ends his speech with a play on words. In order for it to make a complete sentence, the last word must be the verb "ask," the accent falling on the second syllable. But if the first syllable were accented (as the manuscripts read), the word would mean "love," a noun in the accusative case and a form used repeatedly throughout this speech. The sentence would then be incomplete and translated as follows: "Thinking I have left something out, if you still desire love..." Sense requires the first reading, but we shouldn't rule out that Lysias plays upon the sound, inviting his audience to imagine that love is necessary, after all, in a "love relationship." For the same word play, see Plato's *Symposium* 199c1. A good number of the phrases and idioms in this speech are found in Lysias but not in such concentration. The length of the sentences in this speech are longer, on average, than those in Lysias; indeed on average they equal the length of sentences in Socrates' second speech in this dialogue. It is unlikely that this speech is actually by Lysias, but rather a clever and not overly kind parody.

[28] Socrates is punning on Phaedrus' name which means "bright." The word he uses here for "lit up" is *ganusthai*, and related to the name of Zeus' lover Ganymede ("Bright plans/counsels") mentioned at 255c.

[29] "A divine source" translates what in Greek says "divine head" (cf. "dear head" at 264a). Language describing divine possession recurs repeatedly throughout the *Phaedrus,* but Socrates' understanding of the nature of this possession changes over the course of the dialogue. At this point in the *Phaedrus,* Socrates' divine possession is still imperfect. See Glossary under *Divine possession.*

Phaedrus: Come. Do you intend to play like this?

Socrates: Do you really think that I am playing, and not deeply serious?

e **Phaedrus**: No, not at all serious, Socrates, but before Zeus, the god of friendship, declare in earnest—could any other Greek make a greater or better speech on the same theme?

Socrates: What! Must you and I praise the speech *for this*—that the speech-maker[30] said what needed to be said—and not merely for the fact that each of its phrases was clear, compact, and well-turned? But if we must do that, it will be necessary for me to concede to you since *that* escaped

235a my attention, worthless as I am in such matters. I was only thinking about its rhetoric, and this, I suspect, even Lysias himself would think hardly sufficient. For he seemed to me, Phaedrus—unless you can show otherwise—to say the same thing two or three times over, as if he was not particularly adept at speaking in depth on the same theme; or perhaps such things did not concern him. In truth, he seemed to me to have a youthful swagger, showing off how he could say the same thing first in one way, then in another, and doing both rather well.

b **Phaedrus**: Rubbish, Socrates; the material was handled extremely well, He didn't leave out any of the items that are naturally implied by the topic, and everything was given worthy treatment, so that no one could add to what he said or say more or say it better.

Socrates: I simply can't agree with you. If I did, a number of old and wise men and women who have spoken or written on the subject would scold me.[31]

c **Phaedrus**: Who are they? And where have you heard anything better on this subject?

Socrates: I can't come up with names right now, but I clearly have heard some. Perhaps it was the beautiful Sappho, or the skillful Anacreon, or even one of the prose writers. What do I call on as my proof, you wonder. My divinely spirited friend, there's a swelling in my chest, and I feel as if I could, against his speech, make a different one, and no worse either. I'm well aware that I myself know nothing about these things, conscious as I am of my own ignorance. I suppose it remains,

d then, that I have been filled by foreign streams from somewhere which have poured into me, through my ears, as into a vessel. But in my stupidity I have even forgotten how and from whom I've heard these things.

---

30 For speech-maker, see the Interpretative Essay (p. 91) and Glossary under *Unskilled speaker;* see notes 37 and 94.

31 Socrates is undoubtedly being ironic, as only in a most guarded way does Socrates (in Plato) find wisdom in ancient writers. Sappho and Anacreon are lyric poets who sing of the sting of love.

Phaedrus: Even so, my most noble friend, you have spoken very beautifully. No need to tell me how and from whom you have heard this,
even if I were to bid you, but go ahead and do what you said: you
promised to give another speech with different arguments, better than
the one in this book and no shorter. And I promise you that, just like
the nine Archons at Athens, I'll dedicate at Delphi a full-sized, gold
image not only of myself but also of you.[32]

e

Socrates: You are the dearest man and truly made of gold,[33] Phaedrus, if
you think I claim that Lysias completely missed the mark and if you
think that I am really capable of making completely new arguments.
Even the worst prose writer has some merit, I suspect. For example, to
begin with, in this speech do you think one could argue that the non-
lover should be favored over the lover without praising the one for
keeping his head and censuring the other for being out of his mind?

236a

At any rate, these are the necessary points. Can other points be made?
Perhaps so, but one must allow these arguments, I think, and even
pardon them. In cases like this, one must not praise the discovery of
the argument but its arrangement. But in cases when speakers introduce non-essential arguments which are difficult to find, one can praise
discovery in addition to arrangement.

Phaedrus: I agree; in my view you have spoken with due measure.[34] Therefore, this is what I'll do in turn: I shall grant the one essential proposition that the lover is sicker than the non-lover. But regarding all the
rest, if you deliver a speech which is fuller and more appropriate than
his, may you be set up as a metal statue, not one cast in bronze but
beaten out with a hammer, and placed next to the statue of the
Cypselids at Olympia.

b

Socrates: Have you taken this seriously, Phaedrus, because in teasing you
I attacked your darling, Lysias? Do you really think that I'll actually
try to exceed his wisdom and skill with a more varied and subtle
speech?[35]

---

[32] According to Aristotle, archons in Athens took an oath upon taking office to
set up a golden statue if they broke the law; cf. *Constitution of Athens* 7.1.

[33] In typical fashion, Socrates turns physical matter into a metaphor of inner
substance. See 228a and Socrates' view about wealth in his prayer to Pan at
the end of the dialogue (279b-c).

[34] For the play upon the idea of measured speech, see the Interpretative Essay
(pages 91-94) and Glossary under *Unskilled speaker*

[35] "More varied and subtle" translates *poikiloteros* (lit. "dappled") (236b). The
positive form of the adjective appears at 277c to describe certain forms of
speech and certain types of soul. Socrates' terminology here conforms with
that in the *Republic* where *poikilos* also describes a complex soul, which is
often drawn to materialistic and inappropriate desires, including pleasure in
a democratic regime, and it once describes a soul with a bestial nature (588c).

Phaedrus: As to this, my dear, you have been trapped by the same wrestling hold you used on me. You've got to speak, no question about it, as best you can. Otherwise we'll be forced to act like vulgar comedians, exchanging jibes. Don't force me to say: "My dear Socrates, if I don't know Socrates, I have also forgotten myself," and "he was coy, acting as if he wasn't eager to speak." But understand that we shall not leave here until you say what you said was on your chest. We're alone here in a deserted place, and I'm stronger than you—and younger. For all these reasons, "take my meaning,"[36] and don't wait to be coerced, but speak voluntarily.

c

d

Socrates: But, my blessed Phaedrus, I'll be a laughing stock, as I—unskilled and improvising on the spot—go up against a fine maker of speeches.[37]

Phaedrus: Don't you see how it is? An end to this mock modesty! I'm pretty sure that I've got something which, when I say it, will force you to speak.

Socrates: May you never say it, then.

Phaedrus: But I shall, and it will be an oath. I swear—and by whom? let's see…how about by this plane-tree here?—I swear, in truth, that if you refuse to deliver your speech in the presence of this tree, I shall never— I mean, never—show you, or report to you, another speech by anyone else.

e

Socrates: Ah, you brute, you've found out how to force a speech-loving man to do your bidding.

Phaedrus: So why this twisting and turning?

Socrates: Now that you have sworn that oath, I'll stop. For, how could I stay away from such banquets?

237a   **Phaedrus**: Speak, then.

Socrates: Do you know how I'll do it?

Phaedrus: How?

Socrates: I'll cover my head up completely and then speak. In that way as I run through my speech as quickly as possible, I won't lose my way in shame when I look at you.

Phaedrus: Just give your speech. As for the rest, do whatever you want.

Socrates: Come, Muses, whether you are called sweet-voiced from the quality

---

36   In "Take my meaning," Paedrus quotes Pindar, frag. 105.1, a famous tag also in Aristophanes' *Birds* (945); cf. Pindar, *Pythian* 3.80.

37   For Socrates' marked use of terms here, see Introduction (pages 91-94) and Glossary under *Unskilled speaker*. For a play upon the word *metrios* in the context of *poietes*, *idiotes*, and Socrates' speech, see note 34. All adjectival forms of *poietes*, on the other hand, clearly mean "poetic" (245a, 248e, 257a, 265b).

of your song or from your sweet Ligurian origins, "begin to sing with me" my fable[38] which this best of men at my side forces me to speak. He's eager that his companion, whom he already thinks is wise and skilled, seem even wiser and more skilled.[39]

There once was a darling boy, a young man really, a very beautiful young man, and he had a great number of lovers.[40] One of them was wily and persuaded the young man that he was not in love with him at all when in fact he loved him no less than the others. When he was making his case, he tried to persuade the young lad that he ought to grant his favors to someone who didn't love him rather than to one who did. His argument went like this:

Above all else, my darling boy,[41] there is only one way to begin if someone means to deliberate successfully. By necessity,[42] he must know what he is deliberating about or he will miss the mark completely. Most people, however, don't realize that they do not know the true essence of an argument. Because they have not reached an agreement at the beginning of an investigation, they proceed as if they know, resorting

---

[38]   Socrates will call this speech a fable (*mythos*) again at 241e, but he uses the same word to characterize the story of the charioteer and the two horses in the palinode (253c). For more on the word, see Glossary under *Fable*.

[39]   In a forced etymology, Socrates plays on the similarity in sounds between *ligeiai*, a common word in archaic poetry meaning "shrill or high-pitched" (rendered here "sweet voiced") used to describe Muses, singers and their songs, and the *Ligurian* race in northern Greece.   "Begin to sing with me" is a common phrase found at the beginning of archaic songs. This is the *only* speech in all of Plato where a speaker calls upon the Muses.

[40]   "Boy" translates *pais*, a word used for child, son, daughter, or slave (of any age), and in sexual terms for one's darling or beloved, who can range in age from fifteen to thirty-five. "A young man" translates *meirakiskos*, which refers to someone in his early twenties who has not yet started a career.

[41]   The "darling boy" addressed in this speech goes unnamed, although it is tempting to think that Socrates is playfully addressing Phaedrus whom once in the dialogue he clearly addresses as *pais* (267c). If so, this speech, as well as Socrates' next speech, may be seen as a form of seduction, as if Phaedrus were the object of Socrates' desire. Socrates, as a lover of wisdom, wishes to seduce Phaedrus' soul, not his body.   Socrates addresses this "boy" at the beginning and end of both his speeches: cf. 237b and 241c, for the first speech, and 243e and 256e, as well as 252b, for the palinode. Cf. *kallipais* at 261a and note.

[42]   "By necessity" here translates *ananke*, "necessity," a word used ten times in this short speech.   Contrary to Lysias who persistently argues by plausibility (i.e., *eikos*) and who is eager to describe a love which is freed from necessity (cf. 231a and 232a), Socrates' argument in this speech is predicated upon necessity, both in terms of the necessary ways to make an argument and of the passions when they rule over reason.

to what seems plausible, when they have agreed neither with themselves or with others. May you and I, then, not suffer what we fault in
others. And since we are engaged in a discussion about whether one
should enter into a friendship with one who loves you rather than with
d   one who doesn't, we should agree upon a definition of love, showing
what it is and what power it has.[43] Then we can look back at the definition and use it as a point of reference, considering whether love brings
harm or benefit.

Everyone knows that love is a form of desire, and we know that
even those who are not in love desire beautiful things. How then shall
we distinguish the one who loves from the one who doesn't? Further,
one must realize that in each of us there are two forces which rule and
guide us and that we follow both wherever they lead. One of them is
our inborn desire for pleasure, the other an acquired opinion in pur-
e   suit of the best.[44] Sometimes the two, lodged within us, agree; at other
times, they quarrel. Then, sometimes one, sometimes the other gains the
upper hand. When right opinion with reason rules and leads toward
238a the best, we call this moderation.[45] But when desire irrationally drags
us toward pleasures and rules over us, we call this excess. To be sure,
excess has many names—many limbs and many forms[46]—and when
one of these forms happens to be preeminent, a person takes its name,
hardly a beautiful or praiseworthy name to have. When the passion
for food, for example, rules over our best reasoning and our other de-
b   sires, we call this gluttony and the person in the grips of this desire,
gluttonous. Or take the tyrannizing passion for wine, which leads a
drinker in that direction; it is clear what name to call him. And in

---

[43]   "What is it?" *hoion estin* (237c8). Socrates' speech on love in the *Symposium*
begins with precisely the same phrasing (cf. 199c7). In both dialogues,
Socrates sets himself apart from previous speakers by beginning with a
definition, the rest of the speech building on that definition.

[44]   "Opinion" translates *doxa*, which in context can be taken as "judgment;"
compare "straight judgment or opinion," *doxa orthe*, in the *Republic*, 4.431cd.
At 253d, it is translated "glory," another of its meanings.

[45]   See Interpretative Essay (p. 82) and Glossary under *Moderation*. Nowhere else
in Plato does Socrates or anyone else qualify the virtue of (mortal) moderation as he does at 256e-257a.

[46]   Here I follow the manuscript reading *polyeides*, "many forms,"—also used
at 270d and 271a—and not the Oxford editor who prints *polymeres* ("of many
parts"), never found in Plato. The manuscript reading brings out more
clearly that many-limbed arrogance, or hybris, is a hybrid creature and it
recalls, perhaps, the multi-formed (*polyplokoteros*) composition of Typhon
(230a), the Centaurs and the other mythic oddities (*atopiai*, 229d). See note
132.

regard to kindred cases of other desires, and the names for those kindred desires—when that desire is ruling for the time being—it is clear how each should be labeled.

It's relatively clear already, I suppose, why all this has been said, but things are altogether clearer if the reason is spelled out rather than left unstated: when passion without reason rules over straight-minded opinion and is itself driven toward the pleasure of beauty, and, further, when this passion is violently moved by kindred desires toward the beauty of the body and is victorious, it takes its name from that very force and is called love.[47]

My dear Phaedrus, do I seem to you, as I do to myself, to be caught in the grip of a divine passion?[48]

c

Phaedrus: There's no question, Socrates; a most uncustomary fluency has seized you.

Socrates: Then keep silent and listen. In fact, the gods do seem to occupy this place; so don't be astonished[49] if I frequently become Nymph-possessed as the speech continues. Even as it is, I'm not far from speaking in dithyrambs.

d

Phaedrus: Very true.

Socrates: You're responsible for that; still, hear the rest. Perhaps the assault might be averted. But this is in the hands of a god; we, however, must turn our attention back to the boy in this speech.

Very well, my brave fellow. We have already described and given a definition of the thing we have been deliberating about. Now, it remains for us to examine what good or ill will plausibly come from a lover or non-lover to the boy who grants him favors. A man who is ruled by desire and is a slave to pleasure contrives—inevitably, I suppose—to reap the greatest possible pleasure for himself from the beloved.[50] For a sick man, anything that offers little or no resistance is sweet, and

e

---

47   *Eros*, the word for love here, is the second to last word in a long and skillfully constructed periodic sentence. For all intents and purposes, Socrates ends his speech with the word *eros*, as Lysias ended his speech with a play on the sound *erota*, and he plays on its meaning as if *eros* derived from *rhome*, force.

48   "To be caught" (238c6) is in the perfect tense in Greek, a tense used to describe a past action whose effect is still felt in the present.~ beautiful

49   This speech will not astonish Phaedrus, but Socrates' palinode will; see 257c2 and 257c5. For "Nymph-possessed" (*nympholeptos*, 238d1), only here in Plato, see Glossary under *Divine possession*. "I'm not far from speaking in dithyrambs" (238d3; cf. 241e2) also links Socrates with Dionysos, dithyrambic song being connected originally with that god.

50   For the first time in the *Phaedrus*, the beloved appears in the singular; see note 18. In this speech, a lover is interested in his "immediate pleasure" (239a) and depriving the beloved of "things most divine."

239a anything that is equal or stronger is hateful. So a lover will not willingly put up with a boyfriend who is stronger or even on equal terms with himself, but he will make him weaker and more needy, always. So, the ignorant are weaker than the wise, the cowardly are weaker than the manly, those incapable of speech-making are weaker than rhetoricians, and the slow are weaker than the quick-witted.

Necessarily, then, either a lover is deprived of his immediate pleasures, or he enjoys and tries to instill evils such as these, whether they are cultivated or innate—and evils still worse than these—which harm
b the boy's mind. A lover can't restrain his jealousy, or his impulse to prevent the boy from attending all sorts of occasions, especially the beneficial ones, where he may best grow into a man. This is cause enough for harm, but the greatest harm occurs when the lover prevents the boy from attending an occasion where he might best refine his thinking. That is the divine love of wisdom, and a lover must necessarily keep his boyfriend far from it, terrified to his marrow that the boy will grow to despise him. And so, a lover schemes to keep the boy totally ignorant and totally fixed on him, the boy being the sort who, in offering the greatest possible pleasure to the lover, would bring the greatest
c possible harm upon himself. Therefore, in no way is it useful for the mind to have as its guardian or companion a man who is in love.

Next one must consider the outward appearance of the boy's body and its care: both what sort of shape the body is in and how the master of that body will care for it, keeping in mind that the master is compelled to pursue pleasure rather than goodness. No doubt, the lover will be seen pursuing a boy who is soft and not vigorous, one who has not been raised in pure sunlight but under mottled shade, who is not accustomed to manly labors and honest sweat but to soft and un-
d manly living, who decks himself out in fancy hues and cosmetics for want of natural color, and who attends to all the other sorts of things which follow along with these ways, things that are obvious to all and unnecessary to outline further. But before going on, we can bring this point to a head: it's the kind of body that in battle and in other moments of great crisis inspires courage in the enemy but fills friends and the lovers themselves with fear.

Since this is now clear, we must go on and discuss what follows
e upon it: whether in our eyes a lover's guardianship and companionship confer good or ill in the matter of property. This much is clear to all, but especially to the lover, that before all else he would pray for the beloved to be orphaned of his dearest and kindliest possessions, those most divine. He would approve that the beloved be deprived of
240a father, mother, relatives, and friends, on the assumption that they hinder and censor his own most pleasurable company with the boy. He further believes that a boy in possession of gold or some other property is

not as easy to win over, nor, once won, as easy to manage. Accordingly, a lover must certainly be jealous of a boyfriend with property and rejoice if the property is destroyed. And, moreover, the lover would pray for his boyfriend to remain wifeless, childless, and homeless for as long as possible, desiring to enjoy the fruits of the boy's sweetness for as long as possible.

There are other evils too, no doubt, but some divine spirit mixed in a moment's pleasure with most of them. For example, a flatterer is a **b** clever beast and a source of great harm, but nature has thrown into the mix a certain pleasure, and one not altogether boorish. Or someone might call a courtesan harmful, and there are many other creatures and practices of this sort, who moment by moment can be very pleasurable. But a lover, in addition to being harmful to his boyfriend, is also just about the most unpleasant creature to spend the day with. As the say- **c** ing goes: "the young delight in the young." This is so, I suspect, because those of like age are attracted to similar pleasures and form friendships from similar experiences—but still even such fellowship reaches a saturation point. Add to this, there is also that compulsion which is always difficult for anyone to put up with but it is especially trying (as if the age difference weren't enough) when a lover forces himself on the beloved. Day and night the older man hangs around with the youth and is never willing to go away, but is driven on by a **d** compulsion and a sting which bring him pleasure and drive him on whenever he sees, hears, touches, or senses the beloved, so that he waits happily on the beloved, hand and foot.

But what about the beloved? What encouragement or pleasures will the sting arouse in him so that he does not become exasperated spending all that time with a lover who is aging and has lost the bloom of youth? There are all sorts of other experiences that are not pleasant **e** even to hear about, not to mention that they are far more difficult to cope with when you are staring in the face of compulsion: for example, being watched suspiciously at all times and in every circumstance, and listening to inappropriate and overblown praises. In the same way, reproaches which are unbearable when the lover is sober become shameful as well when he is drunk and gives way to excessive and unchecked language.[51]

---

[51] Excessive "language" translates *parresia*, a word which is clearly being used in a pejorative sense here, but which the Athenians often used in a positive sense to refer to the democracy's "freedom of speech or frankness." See Plato's *Republic* 557b; Isocrates 8.14; Euripides' *Hippolytus* 422. Socrates' use of the word here has unmistakable political overtones.

And more: the lover, when in love, is harmful and unpleasant, but when he has ceased loving he is untrustworthy from that moment forward. With endless oaths and entreaties and promising all sorts of things, he was just barely able to sustain the fellowship then, painful as it was, by hope of good things to come. But when he stops loving and has to pay up, he adopts a different principle for himself and a new champion, mind and moderation replacing love and madness, while it has totally escaped the boy's notice that the lover has become a different person. The boy, however, demands return for past favors, remembering what has been said and done before, as if he were talking with the same person. But the lover feels shame and has little courage to say that he is now a different person or that he cannot honor the promises and oaths of his former mindless regime, now that he is a mindful and moderate person. Because he fears he'd revert to his former self if he were to do the same things as he did before. So by necessity the former lover defaults and flees from his promises and in a flip-flop, as if "heads" had become "tails,"[52] takes to his heels.

Having completely failed to realize from the start that he should never have yielded to a lover and to one who is perforce mindless, the boy calls upon the gods in his anger and feels compelled to pursue. Far better it would have been for the boy to submit to a non-lover and a mindful person. Otherwise, it would be necessary for him to surrender to a person who is by nature untrustworthy, fretful, jealous, unpleasant, harmful to his property, harmful to his body, and especially harmful to the education of his soul, than which surely nothing is or ever will be more esteemed, whether by humankind or the gods.

So, keep these things in mind, my darling boy, and understand that a lover's friendship does not stem from kindness but from a kind of hunger and desire for satiety: as wolves adore[53] lambs, so lovers are fond of a boy.

That's it, Phaedrus. You'll hear no more from me, but let this speech find its end here.

Phaedrus: And yet I thought you were half way through, and about to give equal time to the non-lover, describing how it is better to grant favors

---

[52] Socrates here alludes to a game where a sherd is tossed into the air, compelling one party to flee, the other to pursue, depending upon which side is up.

[53] Socrates may be echoing a proverb or drawing from a passage in Homer's *Iliad* 22.262-63: "trusted oaths don't exist between men and lions; nor do wolves and lambs have like minds." This sentence contains the three words for love: *agapao* (adores), *phileo* (am fond of), *erastai*, lovers, from *eraomai*, the word for sexual love used most in the *Phaedrus*. See Glossary under *To Love*.

to him and outlining his good points. But, as it is, why are you stopping, Socrates?

Socrates: Didn't you realize, my blessed fellow, that I am no longer speaking in dithyrambic verse but epic hexameter, even though I am blaming the lover? If I begin to praise the non-lover, what verse form do you think I'll produce?[54] Don't you see that I shall obviously be possessed by these Nymphs whom you deliberately thrust in front of me?[55] Therefore, in a word, I say that whatever we've already said in reproach of the one, the opposite holds true of the other—all good things. Why make a long speech of it? About both, enough said. So my fable will experience whatever fate it deserves, and I think I'll make my way across this river and depart before you force me[56] to say anything more.

Phaedrus: Fine, but not yet, Socrates, at least not before the burning heat of the day passes. Don't you see it's almost exactly noontime when the sun stands still, as they say? Let's wait and continue our discussion, and leave soon when it cools down.

Socrates: You're truly divine when it comes to speeches, Phaedrus, simply astonishing. Of all the speeches that have been made during your lifetime, I'd say no one has produced more of them than you,[57] whether you were the one speaking, or in one way or another you forced others to speak. Your only rival is Simmias of Thebes; and now once again you seem the agent for another speech.

Phaedrus: What good news. But how is that? In what way?

Socrates: Just as I was about to cross the river, my good man, that daimonic spirit and its customary sign came to me; it always restrains me when I'm about to do something wrong. And I thought I heard some voice all of a sudden which would not allow me to go away before I purified myself, as though I had committed some offence or other against

---

54 Dithyrambic verse is lyric, sung by choruses; epic is dactylic hexameter, a meter which Socrates approximates in the last line of his speech.

55 Socrates says that he shall have gods within (the future of *enthousiazo*, 241e, from which verb we get the word "enthused"), but he will realize soon enough that the speech he just gave was a "fault against the divine" (242c). The verb *enthousiazo*, however, continues to be used in Socrates' second speech to describe those enthused with a god (of erotic madness) within. For the instances of *enthousiazo* in the *Phaedrus*, see 241e (here), 249d, 249e, 253a, 263d; also see the adjectival form *entheos* modifying *philos* (255b; cf. 244b). Related to the question of having a god within, is the view that certain speeches are "possessed with soul," *empsukhos*, and others are not.

56 Compare 240c.

57 In the *Symposium*, Phaedrus is called "the father of the discussion" (177d), as the idea of the contest of speeches was his. Also see 270b-d, and esp. 278a-b.

the divine. I am really, then, a prophet, although not an entirely serious one, but just like people who are poor readers, I'm good enough for my own purposes. Clearly I am already learning what my offense is. As you know, my friend, the soul also is prophetic in a way, for she was causing me some trouble even before as I was delivering my speech and I felt shame somehow, lest, in the words of the poet Ibycus,

d   "bringing harm upon the gods, I win honor among men."

And now, I have realized my offense. [58]

Phaedrus: And what is that?

Socrates: It was a terribly clever speech, Phaedrus, a terribly clever speech which you carried with you, and also the one you forced me to speak.

Phaedrus: In what way?

Socrates: The speech was simple-minded, even slightly irreverent; what could be more terrible than that?

Phaedrus: Nothing, if you speak the truth.

Socrates: What else? Don't you believe that Eros is a god, the son of Aphrodite?

Phaedrus: So it is said, to be sure.

Socrates: But not so for Lysias, at any rate, nor for your speech, which was
e   delivered through my mouth while I was drugged and under your spell. But if Eros exists, as in fact he does, whether as a god or at least as something divine, he could not be bad in any way, although both speeches spoke just now as if he were. So in this way they erred about Eros, and on top of that both were simple-minded although very re-
243a   fined, saying nothing salutary or true but putting on airs as if they were,

---

[58] This passage has caused translators considerable difficulty, in part because Socrates at first seems so indefinite about the nature of his offense or even if he has committed an offense and in part because Socrates appears to repeat himself after Ibycus' verse when he says (again) that he has learnt his offense. If we pay close attention to the verb tenses, both problems seem to clear up. In the first instance (242c6), the verb is in the present tense and could be translated "I am learning." Most translators take the word "clearly" in this sentence to mean: "Now, I clearly understand," but the position of the adverb suggests rather "Clearly now, I understand" or "I am learning." The second verb (242d2) is in the perfect, signifying a completed action which still bears upon the present, and is translated here "And now, I have realized." Socrates moves from uncertainty to understanding *after* he recalls Ibycus' verse, yet another instance in the dialogue when poetry shows Socrates the way. Socrates was unique in believing that he had a private divine spirit who appeared only to him, usually in the form of a voice, when he was about to commit an offense against the gods.

trying to deceive a few little human folks and win their praise. Therefore, my friend, I need to be cleansed. Long ago there was a cleansing rite for those who erred when telling fables, one not known to Homer but familiar to Stesichorus. Made blind because he slandered Helen's name, he, unlike Homer, did not fail to understand the reason why. Inspired by the Muses, he recognized the cause and immediately composed the following:

> This account (*logos*) is not genuine[59]—
> nor did you set sail on the well-benched ships,
> nor did you reach Troy's high citadel.

b

And once he composed this so-called Palinode, he immediately regained his sight. So I shall be wiser than both of them in just this one regard. Before I suffer at all on account of my slander of Eros, I shall try to make amends with a palinode, keeping my head bare this time and not covered as before in shame.

Phaedrus: There could be no words sweeter to my ears than these, Socrates.

Socrates: In fact, my good Phaedrus, you too recognize how shameless those speeches were, both the one from the book and the next one. If someone of noble and gentle character happened to hear us saying that lovers get very irate over trivial matters and that they feel jealousy and ill-will toward their boyfriend, and if this someone was either in love with a character like himself or had once been loved, how could you think that he would not believe that he was listening to people who had been raised among sailors and had never seen a noble form of love among the free? And he would be far from agreeing with our censure of Eros.

c

d

Phaedrus: Most likely, by Zeus, Socrates.

Socrates: Accordingly, I am ashamed before this man, and in fear of Eros himself. I wish to wash away such bitter and brackish speech with sweet, fresh words, and I advise Lysias as well to write with haste that one must grant favors to a lover rather than a non-lover, everything else being equal.

Phaedrus: Rest assured that this will be done: once you have offered your

---

[59] The Greek for "genuine" is *etymos*, a word found commonly in Homer but found only three times in all of Plato's writing, all by Socrates in this dialogue (and always in the context of Doric speakers). In all three instances it appears to correct popular opinion: the first at 243a8 when Socrates quotes Stesichorus against Homer's view that Helen went to Troy; the second at 244a3 when Socrates repeats Stesichorus' verse to record his own correction of Lysias' comments about love; the third at 260e5 when a Spartan criticizes the view that rhetoricians only need to concern themselves with public opinion. See note 104.

e   praise of the lover, I shall insist that Lysias write again on the same
theme.[60]

Socrates: I believe you, so long as you are the man you are.

Phaedrus: Take courage, then, and speak.

Socrates: Where's the boy with whom I was just speaking? He must hear
this speech, too, and not be in a rush to grant favors to the non-lover
before he has heard me out.

Phaedrus: That boy's right here, always right by your side whenever you
want him.[61]

244a **Socrates**: You need to understand, my beautiful darling boy, that the former
speech belonged to Phaedrus, the son of Puthokles, from the deme of
Murrhinous in Athens, but what I'm about to say belongs to
Stesichorus, the son of Euphemos, from Himera.[62] It must go like this:
it is not a "genuine account" if it claims that one ought to grant favors
to a non-lover rather than to a lover who is near at hand, just because
one is of sound mind, and the other is mad.

If madness were simply bad, all would be fine. But as it is, the
greatest of all good things come to us through madness, provided that
the madness is divinely given. First, the prophetess at Delphi and priest-

b   esses at Dodona do many good things for Greece, in private and public matters, when they are mad, but when they are of sound mind and
self-controlled they do next to nothing for our country. If we were to
add the Sibyl and all the others who while possessed foretell many
things to many people and guide them toward the future on a straight
path, we would become tedious, detailing the obvious. Yet, it is also
worthwhile to call upon the ancients as witnesses: as their names for
things show, they did not think that madness was a cause for shame

c   or blame. Otherwise, they would not have interwoven the word for
madness, *mania*, into *manike*, the word for that most ennobling art, the
art of expounding the future.[63] But recognizing that *mania* is beautiful
when mixed with a divine portion, they called prophecy "manic,"

---

60   Phaedrus' thoughts are still primarily on rhetoric.

61   Friedlander argues that Socrates "unmistakenly addressed (this speech) to
Phaedrus himself" in what Socrates understood to be a war between sophistic and philosophical rhetoric. Others believe that the erotic banter here
is merely playful.

62   Stesichorus is a real person from Himera, although his name ("Chorus-Mas-
ter") and that of his father ("Good at Speech") may be *noms de plume*. It is
one of those beautiful gifts of language that he is from Himera ("Land of
Desire"), a word Socrates makes much of later in the palinode. See 251bc
and note 78.

63   See Glossary under *Art*. "Most ennobling" translates the word *kalliste*, a
superlative form of *kalos*, "beautiful" or "noble."

whereas people today tastelessly add a "t" and call prophecy the "mantic" art. In the same vein when the search into the future involved level-headed men consulting birds and other signs, the ancients called this an "*oionoistic*" art in the belief that from discursive thinking (*dianoia*) it uses mind (*nous*) and inquiry (*historia*) with human intelligence (*oiesis*), but nowadays the young, solemnly making the "o" long, call the art "oionistic."[64] Just as the "mantic" art is more perfect and honored than the "oionistic" art, both in name and activity, so also madness itself, as the ancients testify, is more ennobling than moderation, the one coming from a god, the other from man.

d

Secondly, in certain families which have been afflicted with the severest diseases and toils from some sort of ancient blood-guilt, madness crops up and prophesies for those in need, finding deliverance. By taking refuge in prayers and service to the gods, madness in conjunction with purifications and secret rites takes him out of harm's way, both for the short term and in the long haul, helping a person who is mad and possessed in the right way, to find a release from present ills.

e

245a

A third form of madness and possession comes from the Muses. This madness takes hold of a tender soul, one pure like a pathless mountain peak;[65] it arouses and fills that soul with a Dionysiac frenzy to make lyric songs and other forms of poetry, the madness arranging and preserving the countless deeds of the ancients for the edification of generations to come. Whoever comes to the doors of poetry without the madness of the Muses, confident that he will become an accomplished poet by skill or art alone, this person and his poetry will fall short of his aim; the poetry of those who are mad will obliterate the poetry of a sound and self-controlled mind.

Such are the beautiful works—and there are more I could tell you about—all products of a god-inspired madness. So, let's not fear madness itself, nor let us be confused by any argument which tries to frighten us into believing that a man of sound mind should be chosen as friend over someone who has been stirred. Rather let that argument carry the day only after it has been shown that the gods do not send *eros* to a lover and the beloved for their benefit. For our part we must

b

---

[64] Making the second "o" long switches the etymology from "understanding" (*no*) with a short "o" to "bird" (*oionos*). Socrates' etymology is, needless to say, fanciful.

[65] "One pure like a pathless mountain peak" translates *abatos* (245a2), a poetic word rarely found in Plato which means "pathless or untrodden," often describing mountain ridges where gods and shepherds roam. Others translate "virgin." Socrates' argument of poetry's benefits for humankind clashes with his views in the *Republic* (387b, 607a), but it should be noted that the virtues of inspired poetry are made here in passing and that poets have a lowly position (sixth out of nine) at 248e.

c   show the opposite—namely that the gods grant such madness for our greatest good fortune. Clever people surely will scoff at this demonstration, but not the wise.

"On the nature of the soul," both in its human and divine forms, it is necessary first of all to consider the truth about what the soul experiences and what her activities are. The demonstration begins as follows.

Every soul is immortal. For the always moving is immortal. And what moves something else and is moved by something else stops living when it stops moving. Only that which moves itself never stops moving, in so far as it never leaves itself, but it is the fount and origin of motion even for other things, however many as are moved. And the

d   origin is ungenerated. For it is necessary that everything which is born come from an origin but the origin does not come from something. If the origin should come from something, it would no longer be the origin. But since the origin is ungenerated, it is also necessarily imperishable. For if the origin is destroyed, neither will it ever be born from something, nor will anything come from it, if it is necessary that all things come from the origin. So, the origin of motion moves itself. It is not possible that it be destroyed or brought into being, or else all of

e   the universe and all that is brought to life[66] would collapse and stand still and never again have the origin from which things find motion. If that which moves itself is called immortal, no one will be ashamed to say that the very essence and account of the soul consists in this. For every body which is moved by an outside source is soulless, but every body which is moved from within by itself is "ensouled," as this is the nature of soul. If it exists in this way, namely that this thing which

246a   moves itself is nothing other than soul, then it would have to be that the soul is both immortal and ungenerated.[67]

Concerning the soul's immortality, then, this is sufficient, but we still need to discuss her form. It would take a god and a long time to examine in every detail what kind of thing the form is,[68] but human beings in a shorter amount of time can describe what she is like. So, let's take this route. Let us liken the soul to the innate power of a winged team of horses and a charioteer. All of the gods' horses and

b   charioteers are themselves good and from good stock, but the situation

---

[66] A variant reads: "all the heaven and all the earth collapses into one."

[67] The style here imitates the language of pre-Socratic, natural philosophers like Parmenides, Herakleitos, Empedocles, and especially Alcmaeon from Croton. Reference to the soul as self-moving links this section with what Socrates says later about love re-installing motion into a wingless soul within a mortal body.

[68] It is equally possible to translate: "to examine in every detail what kind of thing the soul is."

of other horses and charioteers is mixed. For us men, first of all, a charioteer rules over and guides a *pair* of horses, and secondly, one of these horses is noble and good and from like stock, but the other is the opposite and from opposite stock. So, for us chariot-driving must be difficult and irksome.

And next, I should try to explain why living creatures are called both mortal and immortal. Every soul takes care of everything which is soulless and she traverses the entire heaven, changing from one form to another. When she is perfect and winged, a soul roams among the stars and governs the cosmos at large. But when she has lost her feathers, a soul is carried along until she lays hold of something solid where she settles in and acquires an earthly body. Because of the power it gains from the soul, this body appears to move itself and is called in sum a living creature, soul and body having been joined. And it is called "mortal." But the term immortal is not derived from any reasoned account. Although we can neither see nor conceive of a god sufficiently, we fashion[69] him nonetheless as an immortal creature of some sort with a body and a soul, the two joined together for eternity. But allow these things, and our discussion of them, to stand in whatever way it pleases the gods.

And let us consider why the feathers fall off a soul and drop away. The explanation is something like this. By its nature the wing's natural capacity is to convey what is weighty upward and to roam among the stars where the race of the gods dwell; and, most of all bodily parts, it has a share in the divine—the divine which is beautiful, wise, good, and everything of this sort. The soul's feathers are especially nourished and increased by these, but diminished and utterly destroyed by shame, vice, and such opposites. So, then, the great leader in heaven, Zeus, takes the lead, driving a winged team, arranging everything thoroughly and taking care of it. An army of gods and daemons follow him, arranged in eleven contingents, because Hestia, goddess of the Hearth, remains alone in the house of the gods. The rest are arranged in a group of twelve, taking their station according to their assigned rank.[70]

Within heaven there are many blessed vistas as well as beautiful pathways which the race of the happy gods traverses, each of the gods

c

d

e

247a

---

[69] In the phrase, "we fashion" (*plattomen*), Plato appears to be punning on his name, as may also be true in regard to the plane tree (*platanos*, 230b3) where the dialogue takes place.

[70] It is not clear in the Greek whether Hestia is among the twelve, or (more probably) a thirteenth god. In Plato's time, the canon of twelve Olympians was not fixed. If Socrates includes Hestia among the twelve, the others would be Zeus, Hera, Demeter, Poseidon, Aphrodite, Athena, Apollo, Artemis, Hephaistos, Ares, and Hermes; if not, then Dionysos or Hades would make the twelfth. No mortal souls chose Hestia as their god.

attending to his own business.[71] Whoever is willing and able can follow behind, since Envy stands outside the space of the divine dance.
But when the gods go to the feast and banquet, they make the steep

b   climb to the arch of heaven's vault, a journey which the gods' chariots
make with ease as they are well-balanced and obedient to the rein. But
other chariots can barely follow. The vicious horse is heavy and to the
extent that it was not trained well it sinks earthward and weighs the
charioteer down. At this point, the soul experiences extreme toil and
struggle. But when those souls which we call immortal[72] reach the

c   summit of heaven, they go to the edge and stand on the rim; there, the
revolving motion carries them around as they stand and gaze on things
outside the heavens [i.e., a vision of the Forms].

None of the poets here on earth have ever sung the praises of this
place beyond heaven, nor will any ever sing of it adequately. But the
hymn goes like this—for we must have the courage to speak the truth,
especially when the true nature of things is our subject. This is the place
of Being, the Being that truly is—colorless, shapeless, and untouchable,
visible to the mind alone, the soul's pilot, and the source of true knowl-

d   edge. Just as a god's discursive thinking is nourished by the mind and
unmixed knowledge, so is the thought of every soul nourished by what
is appropriate for her to receive. When much time has passed and she
looks upon Being, she feels adoration,[73] and when contemplating the
truth, she is easily nourished and feels joyous, until the revolving
motion carries her around in full circle to the originating point. In this
circuit, the soul looks upon Justice itself, and she looks upon Moderation, and she looks upon Knowledge, but not the knowledge where
Becoming resides, nor the knowledge which changes from object to

e   object regarding things which down here we call Being. Rather, it is
the knowledge of the Being which really is. And once she has similarly looked upon and banqueted on other things which really are, she
re-enters heaven, returning home. When she arrives, the charioteer takes
the horses to the manger, providing nectar for feed and ambrosia for
drink.

248a   Such is the life of the gods. But of the other souls, one follows a
god very well and patterns herself after him, raising up the head of
her charioteer to peer upon the place outside heaven, and she is carried around with the gods in the revolving motion, but even so, this

---

71   In the *Republic*, everyone tending to his own business is the definition of
justice for those who live in the city of speech.

72   A difficult phrase as every soul is immortal. Perhaps Socrates means that
the souls of the gods are immortal in body as well as "in soul."

73   "Feels adoration" translates *agapa* (247d3); see Glossary under *To Love* and
note 53.

soul gets confused by the horses and is scarcely able to gaze upon the things that are. Another soul, harassed by the horses, rises and falls, seeing some things and not seeing others. But all of the remaining souls seek the upward path and are eager to follow but they lack the means and are carried around below the surface, trampling each other and getting smashed about, each one trying to get in front of the other. Confusion and rivalry and great quantities of sweat are the result, some souls being maimed because of the charioteers' wrongdoing,[74] while other souls have their wings shattered. In spite of this great effort, all souls, everyone of them, leave the sight of Being, unfulfilled,[75] and, once departed, feed on the food of conjecture.

The reason for this great haste to see the Plain of Truth and find its whereabouts is that the pasturelands there happen to be just right for the best part of the soul, and that the wing which makes it possible for the soul to become airborne is nourished thereby.

Now, the law of Compulsion. If any soul is in the company of a god and perceives something of the truth, she is free from pain until the next cycle begins; if she is always able to do this, she will always be safe. But whenever a soul cannot see the truth and is thus unable to follow the path, and by some misfortune gets weighed down burdened by forgetfulness and wrongdoing, and in her heaviness sheds her feathers and falls to earth, then the following law applies. In the first generation of a soul's fall to earth, she can never be planted into a brute animal, but the soul which has witnessed Being the most in heaven shall be planted into the seed of someone who will become a lover of wisdom, or a lover of beauty, or of something musical and erotic. The second best soul shall be planted into the seed of a future law-abiding king or a military man, or a ruler; the third best, into the seed of a political man, or an estate manager, or a money-maker; the fourth best, into the seed of one who loves toil, or a gymnast, or a doctor; the fifth best, into the seed of a prophet or seer or priest of mystic rites. In the sixth best soul a poet resides, or someone concerned with imitation; in the seventh, a craftsman or farmer; in the eighth, a sophist or demagogue; in the ninth, a tyrant. In all these men, the one who lives justly has a better portion; the one who lives unjustly, a worse portion.

It takes each soul 10,000 years to return to the same spot whence she started—for the wings don't grow back before then—unless it is **249a**

b

c

d

e

---

[74] "Wrongdoing" translates *kakia*; it could also be translated "cowardice" or "wickedness."

[75] "Unfulfilled" (*ateleis*) could also be translated "uninitiated." Some find this account intentionally humorous or absurd.

the soul of a person who loves wisdom without deceit, or loves a boy at the same time as he loves wisdom. If in the third 1,000 year circuit these souls choose the same life three times in succession, they sprout wings in the 3,000th year and depart. But the rest are judged after their first life is completed; and, once judged, they either go to a house of correction under the earth where they pay their penalty, or, made airborne by Justice, they go to a place in the heavens and live a life wor-

b   thy of the one they lived in their human form. In the 1,000th year both types of souls arrive at a place of allotments where they choose their second life according to their wishes. At that time two things may occur: a human soul could move into an animal life, or a soul, formerly human but now animal, could move back to a human. This is because only a soul which has seen the truth can enter into our human form: for a human being must understand what is said in reference to form,

c   that which, going from a plurality of perceptions is drawn together by reasoning into a single essence. This process occurs by recollecting those things which our soul once saw when traveling in the company of a god, looking with contempt at those things which we now say exist, and lifting up its head to see what really is. As is just, only the discursive thinking of a philosopher, the one who is in love with wisdom, grows wings. For thought is always, according to her capability through memory, near to those things, and by this nearness a god is divine. And only a man who correctly handles such reminders and is perpetually initiated into these perfect mysteries is truly perfect. But

d   standing apart from zealous human pursuits and being near to the divine, he is admonished by the many for being deranged, because they fail to see that he is divinely possessed, having the god within.

Certainly, then, everything about our fourth madness is here: when someone looks upon earthly beauty and is reminded of the true beauty, he acquires wings; and when he tries those wings, eager but unable to take flight—like a bird looking upward—and he shows no concern for things below, there are reasons to think him touched with madness.

e   Both for the person who has this madness and for the one who shares in it, this is the very best of all the divine possessions, and it comes from the best sources; and the lover hit with this madness is called a lover of beautiful people and beautiful things. And, as we have said, by our very nature every human soul has already viewed the things

250a which are; or else she wouldn't have come into this life form.

But it is not easy for every soul from her earthly perspective to recall those distant things, especially for those souls which saw them briefly or had bad luck when falling here, so that when they were turned toward injustice by some company or other here they naturally forgot the sacred things they had seen there. To be sure, few souls are left for whom that memory is sufficient. Whenever they behold an image of the things there, they are thoroughly startled and they are no longer themselves and they do not recognize the sensation that they are having because they cannot perceive it sufficiently. There is no shine   **b** in the images here on earth of justice and moderation and the other things honorable for souls, but through the dim organs of the senses a few people, and they with difficulty, approach these images and behold the original of the thing imaged. Formerly, however, it was possible to look upon beauty in its radiance when in a blessed chorus-dance we in Zeus' entourage, and others in the company of other gods, witnessed a blest sight and spectacle and we were initiated into what it is lawful to call the most blest of the mysteries. Celebrating these   **c** inspired rites, we were whole and untouched by those evils which lay in wait for us later. Being fully initiated and looking upon whole, simple, unchanging, and blessed visions[76] in pure light, we were ourselves pure and unmarked by what we now carry around and call a body, a thing which imprisons us like an oyster shell.

the body imprisons /the soul

Let this tribute to memory be agreeable, a tribute which we have lingered over for some time in our longing for things past. But now, as we were saying, beauty shone brightly in the midst of those visions.   **d** And when we came here, we grasped it shining most clearly through the clearest of our senses, because sight is the sharpest of our physical senses. But thought is not seen by it—oh, what awe-inspiring loves sight would provide if it could provide just as clear an image, as beauty does, of thought itself or of other lovely forms. But, as it is, beauty alone has this distinction to be naturally the most clearly visible and the most   **e** lovely.

Thus, the person who has been corrupted or who is not a recent initiate is not conveyed quickly to beauty itself, that is, he is not carried from here to there quickly. When looking at beauty's namesake here, such a person fails to experience true reverence as he gazes but yields to pleasure and tries to mount and to spawn children according to the law of a four-footed animal. In company with wantonness, he shows no fear or shame as he pursues unnatural pleasure. But the recent ini-   **251a** tiate, someone who has amply observed things from that past realm, at first shudders and feels something of those old terrors come over him when he sees a god-like face or any part of the body which is a good imitation of beauty. Later, looking more, he feels reverence as if he were

---

[76] "Visions" translates *phasmata*, an extremely rare word in Plato and only here in the *Phaedrus*. Socrates uses the language of initiation to describe "sight" of the Forms themselves, although, by definition, they belong to the invisible realm of Being and not to the physical realm of Becoming. Forms cannot be perceived with the senses, nor can divine beauty be seen with the eyes, but only a copy or likeness (*eidolon*) of it in the figure of a beautiful body or person. See Glossary under *Form(s)*.

before a god and, if he were not afraid to appear excessively mad, he would sacrifice to his darling boy as if to a statue and a god. As is natural after his cold shudder, a change, accompanied by sweat and unaccustomed fever, comes over him as he looks. At the same time, he is warmed as he receives the in-flowing of beauty through the eyes. From the in-flowing, the natural power of the wing is watered and with this warmth the scabbing around the projection which sometime before had hardened and closed up, preventing blooming, begins to melt away. With the in-flowing nourishment the wing's stalk under the surface of the soul begins to swell and to feel the urge to grow from its roots. At one time, you know, the entire soul was winged.[77] In this state the whole soul boils and throbs violently—not unlike the itching and aching irritation around the gums that a child feels when he begins to teethe. That's the same sensation which the soul feels when her wings begin to sprout: she boils, aches, and itches. So, whenever a soul looks at a boy's beauty she is watered and warmed from this as she takes in these in-flowing and invading draughts of beauty—that's why it's called "desire."[78] This causes both a relief from pain and a feeling of joy.

But when the soul is separated and feels dry, the openings of the passageways through which the feathers have pushed are closed and

[77]   It is very probable that "winged" is slang for the erect phallus, a point made even more strongly at 252b. In the prior sentence, "stalk" translates *kaulos*, a word only used here in Plato's *oeuvre*. It refers principally to the stalk of a plant and here is frequently translated as "quill"; the word is also widely used to refer to the duct of a penis, a woman's cervix, or the penis itself. With other words in this passage referring to growth, swelling, and pulsing, it appears as if the double entendre is fully intended. The philosophic soul's eroticism is contrasted with the corrupt soul's "unnatural" desire to beget children. Unlike the aroused penis of a corrupt soul which can find a physical object to relieve its desire, the aroused state of the philosophic soul can only be relieved by a "recollection" or "memory" of the eternal Forms. In the *Republic* 490b5, a lover is said to "couple with" (*migeis*) the Forms, the union begetting intelligence and truth and a cessation from the labor (of childbearing) (*odines*, the first meaning of which is "the throes of childbirth").

[78]   The alliteration of "draughts" and "desire" attempts to capture Socrates' play on words when he offers an etymology: *himeros* ("desire") from *mere*, "parts or portions," and *rheonta*, "flowing." A more literal translation is as follows: the soul is warmed by "receiving portions (*mere*) which come and flow in (*epionta kai rheonta*) from there—which is why it is called desire (*himeros*)." For Stesichorus from Himera in whose voice Socrates delivers this speech, see 244a and note 62; and for Himeros as the name of the spring which Zeus associates with his love for Ganymede, see 255c, and note 86. Also 253a. For a different Platonic etymology of *himeros*, see the *Cratylus* 420a. At 249e, there seems to be a different etymological word play, deriving *erastes* ("lover") from *ho eron* ("the lover") and *aristos* ("the best").

dried up, shutting off the budding of the feather. When this has been shut off with desire locked in, the unborn feather throbs like pulsing arteries, each pricking at its passageway, so that the entire soul is actually stung all over, driven mad with anguish; but when she recalls the beautiful boy again, she feels joy.

When both sensations are intermixed, the soul is both greatly troubled by the oddity of the experience and raves, at a loss to understand it. Driven mad, she is neither able to sleep at night nor remain in one place by day, but, yearning she runs to whatever place she thinks she will see the boy who possesses beauty. When she has seen him and is bathed in the waters of desire, she loosens those places previously jammed tight and, free from the stings and birth pangs, she draws in a big breath, and once again reaps the fruits, for a moment, of this most sweet pleasure. She is not willing at all to be deprived of this pleasure, nor does she consider anything more valuable than this beautiful boy; but has already forgotten mothers, brothers, and all her companions. She thinks nothing of losing property through neglect and spurns all habits and refinements by which she beautified herself before, ready now to be a slave and to sleep wherever she is permitted so long as it is very near the object of her desire. In addition to revering the boy who possesses beauty, the soul finds in him the only doctor for her greatest labors and pains.

My beautiful darling boy, this passion which we have been discussing, human beings call love; but when you hear what the gods name it, you will laugh probably because of your youth. Some Homeric singers, I think, speak of two verses from an unpublished epic to Love, and one of them is utterly outrageous and not entirely metrical. But the song goes like this:

> Verily mortals call him winged Eros,
> but gods call him Winged, because he makes things rise.[79]

We may or may not trust these verses, but the characteristics and the experience of lovers are just like this.

---

[79] The gods fuse noun and adjective, calling "winged Eros" (*eros potenos*) "Winged" (*Pteros*), *pteros* used only here and in its adjectival form at 251b7 in Plato. As already suggested in 251a-d, Socrates is probably drawing on a common portrait of the erect penis in Greek art as winged, what in English might be rendered a Winged Pecker or a Cock. For "He makes things rise" which translates *pterophytor' ananken* (literally: "wing-making compulsion"), I thank my student Collomia Charles. See further, William Arrowsmith, "Aristophanes' *Birds*: The Fantasy Politics of Eros," *Arion* n.s.1 (1973) 119-67, esp. Appendix II on the *Phaedrus*, pp. 164-67, an argument made stronger if *kaulos* is added to the discussion. No doubt, it is the gods' use of slang which causes the young to laugh.

If a man who has been seized by love was once among Zeus' entourage, he is able to bear the burden of winged compulsion with a good deal of dignity. But those who were in Ares' camp and traveled the circuit with him—if they are captured by Love and for any reason suspect that they've been wronged by their darling boy, they become

d homicidal and are ready to sacrifice themselves and the beloved. Each walks in the footsteps of the god he chooses, joining in that choral dance, living out his life in honor of that god, and imitating him to the best of his abilities for as long as he remains uncorrupted and is in his first incarnation here on earth. He behaves this way to all: both to those he loves[80] and to everyone else. Each person, then, chooses his Love from among the beautiful after his own tastes, and sculpts and

e fits that person out like a statue as if he were a god for him to honor and to worship with secret rites.

The followers of Zeus search for a beloved who is noble and Zeus-like in his soul, and they ask whether the beloved is by nature a lover of wisdom and a ruler. Whenever they find him, they fall in love and do everything they can to help him become such a person. But if lovers have not practiced this kind of service before, they now try their hand at it and learn from any source, finding their way on their own.

253a As they follow the scent and search within themselves to discover the nature of their god, they have an easy time of it because they are fiercely driven to gaze upon the god. And in this way when they make contact with a god through memory, they are possessed by him and pick up his habits and practices to the extent that humans can share in the divine. As they attribute the cause of these feelings to the beloved, they adore him even more dearly; and, if they draw their inspiration from Zeus, then like inspired Bacchants[81] following Dionysos they pump this

b inspiration into the beloved's soul and make him as similar as possible to their god.

Those who follow Hera, in turn, seek a beloved who is regal in nature, and if they find him they do all the same things for him. Followers of Apollo and each of the other gods, proceed in the manner of their god and search for a boyfriend whose nature resembles their god; when they acquire him they themselves imitate the god and persuade and discipline the darling, leading him into the service and ways of the god, according to each one's ability. They do so without envy or

c stingy ill-will toward the darling but in the hope that, trying as hard

---

[80]   As mentioned in note 20, outside Lysias' speech this is the one place where "beloved" is in the plural.

[81]   Bacchants, filled with the god Dionysos (not Zeus), like lovers are possessed by a divine frenzy. There is a contagion about this frenzy to which all in the god's company are susceptible. See notes 29 and 49.

as they can, they may lead the loved one wholly and entirely to re-
semble both themselves and the god whom they honor. The eagerness
of those truly in love and the initiation rite, if lovers obtain what they
are eager for in the way I have outlined, become both beautiful and
blessed. It is a blessedness which derives from the love-crazed friend
but also benefits the boy who is befriended, provided, that is, the boy
is captured. And this is how to conquer the one who is captured.

Just as at the beginning of our fable we divided each soul into
thirds—two parts, horse forms of some sort; the third, the form of a
charioteer[82]—let's continue to use them even now for our story. One of   **d**
the horses, we said, was good, the other not, but we haven't discussed
the excellence of the good one or the vice of the vicious one. We should
do that now. Well, of the two, one stands in the position of greater
beauty (i.e., on the right), in form erect and well-jointed, high-necked,
hooked nose, white to behold, black-eyed, a lover of honor with a sense
of moderation and shame and a companion of true opinion, without
need of the whip, ruled by command and word alone. But the other is   **e**
crooked, bulky, poorly slung together, stiff-necked, thick-necked, snub-
nosed, black-skinned, cloudy-eyed, hot-blooded, a companion of wantonness and insolences, shaggy about the ears, obtuse, and scarcely
obedient to whip or goad.[83] Therefore, whenever the charioteer beholds
the eyes of his beloved—the sensation having thoroughly warmed the
whole soul—and he begins to feel a tickling and a desire for the goad,   **254a**
the obedient horse, constrained as always by a sense of shame,[84] restrains itself from jumping upon the darling boy. But the other horse
no longer minds the charioteer's goad or the whip as it bounds up and
is carried along by force. It causes every kind of difficulty for its yoked
partner and for the charioteer, forcing them to move toward the darling boy and to recall the delight of sex. At the beginning, the two re-

---

[82] "Form(s)" translates *eide* (plural), *eidos* (singular), the same word used for
the invisible Forms of true Being. See Glossary under *Form(s)*.

[83] Socrates' vocabulary to describe these two creatures ("horse forms of some
sort") parallels but is unlike any other description of horses in Greek literature, as my student Collomia Charles has observed. Socrates' description
falls into three categories: deportment, temperament, and beauty; it seems
likely that they reflect traits of the human soul. "Of right opinion" could
also be translated "of true and good reputation"; "stiff necked" more literally is "strong necked" (a sign of stubbornness in horses); "cloudy-eyed"
more literally is "gray eyed" (but only horses with cataracts have gray eyes;
but perhaps "blue-eyed" is meant, a sign of weak vision); "insolences" could
also be translated "false pretenses"; "obtuse" is usually translated "deaf" (a
translation made difficult by 254d-e), and here refers to a thick-skinned horse,
unresponsive to the whip.

[84] This could also mean "pressing hard in accord with a sense of shame."

b sist and are irritated, feeling forced to engage in terrible and unlawful acts, but finally when they find no end to this vice they follow along passively, both of them yielding and agreeing to do whatever is commanded.

They approach the boy and see the darling's face, flashing like a lightning bolt. With this sight the charioteer's memory is carried toward the essence of the beautiful, and once again he sees beauty itself standing alongside moderation on a holy pedestal. Overcome with fear and reverence by the sight, the charioteer's memory recoils on its back and

c is compelled simultaneously to pull back on the reins with such violence that both horses naturally sit on their haunches, one willingly because it does not resist, but the wanton one extremely unwilling. When both withdraw some distance from the boy, one from a sense of shame and astonishment bathes the entire soul with sweat; the other, having scarcely regained its breath and no longer feeling pain from the bit and the fall, starts in a fury to abuse and to curse the charioteer and its yoke-mate excessively for cowardice and lack of manliness for

d having abandoned their station and their agreement. Forcing them against their will to advance again, the black horse steps back, but barely, as they plead to put off the advance for a time. But when that agreed-upon time is up and the other two pretend to have forgotten, it reminds them both: forcing, snarling, dragging, it makes them approach the darling again to deliver the same words, and when they are near, it pulls forward, head down, tail straight back, biting on the bit, shame-

e less. Even more resentful than before, the charioteer falls back as if recoiling from a starting gate, still more violently yanking back on the bit in the wanton horse's mouth. Bloodying its abusive tongue and jaws, he presses the legs and haunches of the horse hard upon the ground in pain. Only when it has suffered this same treatment repeatedly does the despicable creature cease its wanton excess. Humbled, in the end it follows the charioteer's plan, and when it sees the beautiful boy it is devastated by fear. Then at last it actually happens that the lover's soul follows the darling with awe and a sense of shame.

255a Because the boy is now waited on in every possible way as if he were a god, and the lover is no longer pretending but truly feels his servitude, the boy is naturally friendly to the one who offers him such attention, even if earlier he thrust away from the lover, when he had been misled by his schoolmates and others who said that it was shameful to be near him. But with the passage of time, his age and necessity

b compel the boy to admit the lover into his company, as it has never been ordained by fate that vice be dear to vice or that good not be dear to good. When the boy admits him, accepting his conversation and

company (or intercourse),[85] the lover's kindness being near now aston-
ishes the boy as he perceives how all his other friends and relatives
put together do not offer a fraction of the friendship of his godly-in-
spired friend. When the lover continues over time to be kind and to
remain by his side, even to the point of touching in the gymnasium
and other places of companionship, a spring, from that flow which   c
Zeus in love with Ganymede called Desire (*Himeros*),[86] gushes over the
lover, part of its waters entering into him and part of it overflowing
when he has become full. As a breeze or perhaps an echo bounces off
a smooth hard surface and is carried back to the source from which it
sprang, just so the flow of beauty goes back into the beautiful one
through his eyes, arriving where it naturally goes into the soul, causing movement of the wing. There the stream waters the pathways of   d
the feathers, urges them to sprout, and fills the beloved's soul in turn
with love.

   The boy is then in love, but he is at a loss to say with what. He
doesn't know what he has experienced, nor is he able to explain it,
but just as a person who has contracted an eye-disease from someone[87]
is unable to name the alleged cause, so he does not realize that in his
lover he is seeing himself as though in a mirror. When that man is near,
his pain ceases, as it does for the man. But when the man is absent,
the boy yearns and is yearned for, again in the same ways, as he experiences a "return-love," an image or copy of love. He calls and consid-   e
ers this to be friendship, not love. Like the man, only less intensely, he

---

[85]   *Homilia* typically refers to social intercourse (as at 239e, 250a, and 255b) but
       it can also mean sexual intercourse, although there is no passage in Plato
       where it must be taken in this vein. Usage here (255b) and at 255b and
       240a leaves room for ambiguity, perhaps deliberately. See *phileo* conveying
       outward (i.e. physical) signs of love at 255e and 256a (note 88). "No longer
       pretending" refers back to 237b.

[86]   The myth of Zeus and the mortal Ganymede parallels the theme of Socrates'
       speech: a descent from Olympus to seize an object of beauty to bring him
       up to Olympus; compare Boreas "blowing down" to "snatch up" Oreithuia
       (229c). For other references to Himera in this speech, see 251c and notes 63
       and 78. By punning on Ganymede's name, Socrates links him to Phaedrus,
       whose name also means "bright"; see note 28. In submitting to a lover, the
       beloved gains friendship (cf. 240d) more than bodily pleasure, though that
       is not absent, as we can see from this passage.

[87]   Eye diseases, the Greeks believed, could be transmitted by looking into in-
       fected eyes.

desires to see, to touch, to kiss,[88] to lie down beside. And then, as is likely, soon afterwards he does these very things.

When the two lie together, the lover's unbridled horse has a word with the charioteer, feeling that it deserves for its many labors some small return; but the darling's vicious horse can't speak a word. Full to bursting[89] and at a loss what to do, it throws itself all over the lover with kisses, and embraces him for being extremely kind. And when they do lie down together, this horse does not intend to hold back any part of himself to the lover if he should beg for sexual favors. The horse's yoke-mate and the charioteer, however, from a sense of shame and reason, resist.[90] So if the better parts of discursive thinking prevail, as they lead toward a regimented life and a love of wisdom, then all involved enjoy a blessed and harmonious life here on earth. Self-composed and master of themselves, they have enslaved what enables viciousness to enter the soul and they have liberated what allows excellence access.[91] When they die, now winged and buoyant they have won the first round of the three wrestling falls in these, the true Olympic Games.[92] There is no greater good than this that either mortal moderation or divine madness can provide a human being.

But if they adopt a more coarse way of life, one that loves honor and not wisdom,[93] then perhaps when drunk or in some other careless hour the couple's two unbridled horses will catch their souls unguarded and lead them forward to the same thing, namely to seize upon and carry out a course of action which many consider most blissful. And when they have carried out this act once, they will continue to do so for the rest of their lives, though sparingly, since they do not approve

[88] Here (255e) and at 256a, the verb *phileo* conveys physical expressions of love, here translated "to kiss"; for the use of the verb in the *Phaedrus*, see notes 12 and 53. The "return-love" (*anteros*) of 255e1 may represent a radical departure from older man and "boy" sexual mores. According to this view, Sappho's love poetry presents a female eroticism of reciprocity and mutuality not found in Greek male same-sex relationships; cf. David Halperin, "Plato and Erotic Reciprocity," *Classical Antiquity* 5 (1986) 66-7. For arguments of comparable reciprocity between males, see the Introduction and Appendix C.

[89] The word for "full to bursting" is *spargon* and is particularly associated with breasts swelling with milk.

[90] The language echoes 253d6-e1 to a degree, where *logos* is translated as "word" rather than "reason;" in this dialogue on speech and word, it is only on rare occasions as here that *logos* is translated as "reason."

[91] In Lysias' speech, by contrast, sexual pleasure was a reward for excellence (*arete*); see 232d. But in this speech, excellence depends upon enslaving sexual appetite.

[92] See 249a. In Olympic wrestling-matches, the third throw brings victory.

[93] In the *Republic*, love of honor is the first indicator that a soul is no longer harmoniously arranged; see (549aff).

of this with their full mind. When in love and later when out of love, these two also go through life as friends with each other, although not so close as the philosophic couple, believing that they have given to each other and have received the greatest pledges which it would be a crime to break and feel enmity. In death, their souls are wingless, and yet they are eager to sprout feathers as they leave their bodies, so that actually they have not carried off a small prize for their erotic madness. It is the law for those who have already begun their journey in lower heaven that they shall not return to the dark path under the earth, but shall lead a bright life in blessed journeys with each other, and from their love shall grow, in due time, common plumage.

d

e

My darling boy, a lover's friendship will bestow upon you these great and divine blessings. But a non-lover's intimacy is diluted by mortal moderation and pays meager mortal benefits. It begets in his friend's soul a slavish economizing which most people praise as a virtue but will cause your soul to roam for 9,000 years around the earth and beneath it, mindlessly.

257a

This, my dear Eros, is the finest and most beautiful palinode within my powers. I offer it to you in atonement. If my phrasing and other things have been rather poetical, understand that Phaedrus has forced them upon me.[94] Pardon what went before and find favor in this; in your kind graciousness, don't take away that erotic art given me earlier, nor in anger maim me, but grant that these beautiful boys value my art still more in the future than now. If in the former speech Phaedrus and I said anything that shocked you, find fault with Lysias, father of the speech, and stop him from making such speeches; rather turn him toward a love of wisdom, just as his brother Polemarchos has already been turned. Do this so that his lover here, Phaedrus, may also stop going in two directions as now,[95] but devote his life solely to Love with wisdom-loving speeches.

b

---

[94] This picks up a point Socrates made at 234c. We must understand irony in the claim that the poetic tones of this speech are for Phaedrus' sake. Nowhere else in Plato does Socrates describe such an esctatic vision, a place beyond heaven never before described by a *poietes*.

[95] The God of Love, we see again, turns a lover and guides him towards philosophy. The point is particularly relevant to Phaedrus whom Socrates describes as "going in two directions" (*epamphoterize*, 257b), wavering as he is between Lysias and Socrates' speeches. In the *Republic*, the verb describes things which are multiples, both beautiful and ugly, big and small, etc. In Aristotle, it is a technical term to describe plants and animals (like apes, monkeys, baboons) which cross between categories. What Aristotle describes in botanical and zoological categories, Socrates in this dialogue describes in mythic terms, as in hybrid creatures like the Centaurs and Typhon who exhibit complex natures (cf. 229d-230a, and note 15).

Phaedrus: I join with you in that prayer, Socrates, if this will really be
c   better for us. But for some time now I have been astonished by your
speech,[96] considering how much more beautifully you turned this
speech than the first one. It's actually made me anxious lest Lysias
seem second-rate by comparison—if, that is, he even wanted to match
your speech with one of his own. In fact, my astonishing man, one of
those public figures in the city was recently haranguing him for this
very thing, throughout his speech referring to him as a "speechwriter."
So for love and honor, he might refrain from writing for us.

Socrates: That's ridiculous, young man, and you are far off the mark about
d   your companion if you really believe that he's so easily frightened by
noise like that. But perhaps you think that the man who was chastis-
ing Lysias meant what he said as a reproach.

Phaedrus: So it seemed, Socrates. And you too are aware, I suppose, that
the most powerful and revered men in a city are ashamed to write
speeches and to leave their written compositions for others to see, fear-
ing that in the future they'll be labeled "sophists."

e **Socrates**: It's like the "Pleasant Bend"[97] in the Nile, Phaedrus. You also
seemed to have forgotten that these self-regarding politicians especially
love to write speeches and to leave their written compositions around.
These are the writers who so adore people who approve of their writings that whenever they write a speech they actually begin by naming
on each occasion those who approve of them.

Phaedrus: What in heaven's name do you mean? I don't understand.

258a **Socrates**: You don't understand that approvals are recorded up front at
the beginning of a politician's text?

Phaedrus: How is that?

Socrates: "It was decreed by the Council," or "by the People," or by both;
so he begins, I suppose. Or "so-and-so said"—in this last case the writer
with great pomp and circumstance referring to himself. And then he
proceeds to show off his own wisdom to those who approve, sometimes making an extraordinarily long text. Or does a written speech
seem to differ from such writing somehow?

---

96   When Socrates interrupts himself in his first speech, he told Phaedrus not to
be astonished by what he was saying (238d2) and Phaedrus complied; but
now he is astonished, even if his attention still seems to be on the competition with Lysias rather than the substance of Socrates' palinode.

97   Even for the generations after Plato, the meaning of "Pleasant Bend" was
lost. Presumably, it refers to a bend in the river, lengthening the distance
between two points. If so, the phrase means the opposite of what it says,
the bend being anything but pleasant and Socrates uses the proverb to suggest that politicians love to write. Others take it as a term of endearment
for Phaedrus.

Phaedrus: No, not at all.   b

Socrates: Therefore, if this speech is approved, the maker of the speech leaves the theater[98] rejoicing; but if it is discarded and he is excluded from the business of speech writing, not being considered a worthy writer, then he grieves, and so do his friends.

Phaedrus: Very true.

Socrates: So it's clear—far from despising this practice, these people really admired it, and are actually astonished by it.

Phaedrus: Yes, absolutely right.

Socrates: Well then—when a man becomes so proficient an orator or a king that he naturally becomes an immortal speech-writer in his city with   c the capacity of a Lykourgos or a Solon, or Darius,[99] doesn't he consider himself godlike when he's alive, and don't future generations believe the same things about him because of his writings?

Phaedrus: Very true.

Socrates: Do you think, then, that such a person—no matter who he is or how disaffected with Lysias he might be—would reproach that man for writing?

Phaedrus: It is not likely from what you are saying, for then he would be reproaching his own passions, it seems.

Socrates: Then this much is clear to all: writing speeches, at least, is not   d in itself shameful.

Phaedrus: And why should it be?

Socrates: But this, I think, is shameful: not speaking or writing well, but doing it shamefully or badly.

Phaedrus: That's it, clearly.

Socrates: How, then, do you write well or poorly? Phaedrus, ought we to cross-examine Lysias about these things, and anyone else who has ever

---

[98] The verbal play in this passage causes translators great difficulty: (Hackforth) "if the speech holds its ground, the *autho*r quits the *scene* delighted"; (Nehamas and Woodruff) "if it remains on the books, he is delighted and leaves *the stage as a poet*"; (Rowe) "if it stays written down, the *author* leaves the *theatre* delighted." The maker of the speech/author/poet=*poietes*; theater/scene/stage=*theatron*.

[99] All three lawmakers were famous for their political innovations or reforms. Lykourgos is legendary founder of Sparta's constitution and military system. Solon was elected *archon* in Athens in 594 BCE to redesign a government in crisis and to help redress the grievances of the poor. Darius, King of Persia from 521-486, was also renowned for his political reforms of an empire in turmoil. Of the three, only Solon was also a poet, but that is not what is stressed here. Nor is his role as poet important at 278c where Solon is grouped with those who write political tracts, and not with poets.

written or intends to write anything, whether it be a political or private written work, whether he writes with measure like a speech-maker or without measure like an unskilled speaker?[100]

e **Phaedrus**: Are you asking if we ought to do this? What would anyone possibly live for—so to speak—if not for such pleasures? It is not, I suppose, for those pleasures which necessarily cause pain before pleasure or else no pleasure at all, a condition which is true for nearly all bodily pleasures, and so are rightly called slavish.

Socrates: Well, we seem to have leisure time now for it. And at the same
259a time the cicadas, singing overhead and conversing with each other as they do in this stifling heat, seem to be looking down on us also. If they should see that the two of us are not talking but, like most men at noontime, are slumbering and bewitched by them because our minds are idle, they would justly laugh at us and believe that we were some slaves coming to a small resting place, like sheep sleeping around a spring at noontime. But if they see that we are conversing and sailing
b past them, as if past Sirens, unbewitched, then perhaps they might admire us and give us the gift of honor which they have from the gods to give to human beings. [101]

Phaedrus: What gift is this? I don't think I've heard of this one.

Socrates: Really? It's unimaginable that a lover of the Muses wouldn't have heard of such things. The story goes that once upon a time before the Muses were born these creatures were human beings, but after the Muses were born and singing was revealed, some people in those days
c were so dumbstruck with pleasure that they just sang, actually taking no interest in food or drink, and they died before they knew what happened. Later, the race of cicadas grew from those human beings and received the following honor from the Muses: to have no need for food when born but straightway, without food or drink, to sing until they die, and then going to the Muses to report back, announcing who

---

[100] The verbal play in this passage exceeds 258b2-3. The passage is more comlex than usually seen. The antithesis of *politikon* and *idiotikon* refers to political and private prose writings. The antithesis of *poietes* and *idiotes* marks a more difficult juxtaposition. Others have translated: "whether *in the verse of the poet or the plain speech of prose*" (Hackforth); whether "*poetic verse or plain rose*" (Nehemas and Woodruff); "whether he writes *as a poet, in verse, or in plain man's prose*" (Rowe). See note 124.

[101] "Small resting place" recalls Socrates' description of the grove as a "resting place" (230b2). In the beginning of the dialogue Socrates said that he had no leisure to consider myths (229e4), a condition which appears to have changed. It is important to note that the cicadas as Sirens signal a danger but as the bestowers of a gift of honor a benefit. Both terms are Homeric; "gifts of honor" reoccurs at 262d5.

on earth honors which one of them. Reporting to Terpsichore those who honor her in the choruses, they make them more dear to her; and they report to Erato those who honor her in erotic matters, and so forth for the other Muses according to the form of each one's honor. But they report to Kalliope with the beautiful voice, the oldest of the Muses, and to heavenly Ourania, the second oldest, those who have gone through life loving wisdom and honoring their musical art; for of all the Muses these two send out the most beautiful voices and are especially fond of heaven and of speeches, both divine and human.[102] For many reasons, then, we must say something and not fall asleep at the noon-hour. **d**

Phaedrus: Yes, then, we must keep speaking.

Socrates: Therefore, we ought to consider the very thing we proposed just now to consider—how one is able to speak and write beautifully, and how not. **e**

Phaedrus: Clearly.

Socrates: Then, isn't it necessary for those who intend to speak well and beautifully to have before all else a discursive understanding of the truth about the subject he means to discuss?

Phaedrus: About this, my dear Socrates, I've heard people say that a student studying to become an orator need not learn what justice really is but merely what it seems to be to the masses who are in the position to pass judgment. Nor does he have to learn what is truly good or beautiful but only what seems so; persuading comes from this, not from the truth. **260a**

Socrates: "The word cannot be cast aside,"[103] Phaedrus, that is, the word which the wise utter, but we must consider whether they are saying something significant. In particular, we can't ignore what you said just now.

Phaedrus: Yes, right.

Socrates: Let's look at the question like this.

Phaedrus: How?

Socrates: If I should persuade you to ward off the enemy by buying a horse and neither of us should know what a horse was, but I happened to know that Phaedrus believed a horse was a tamed animal with very large ears... **b**

---

[102] For divine and human narratives, see 246a. Divine speech, no doubt, discusses the thing itself, whereas human speech must rely upon images and myth. Inspiration and mantic speech blur these distinctions and through them, as perhaps through a love of wisdom, human *logoi* may include something of divine *logoi*.

[103] Socrates is quoting Nestor from *Iliad* 2.361.

Phaedrus: Socrates, this would be ludicrous.

Socrates: Not quite yet, but it would be ludicrous if in all seriousness I should persuade you by fabricating a speech in praise of an ass, calling it a horse and claiming that the creature is invaluable at home and on campaign, suitable to fight from and to carry equipment and many other things besides.

Phaedrus: This would be totally ludicrous.

Socrates: But isn't it better to be ludicrous and friendly, rather than clever and hostile?

Phaedrus: So it seems.

Socrates: So, when a rhetorician who is mindless of good and evil encounters a city in the same condition and attempts to persuade it, not by praising a mere shadow of an ass as if it were a horse but by praising evil as good, and by carefully studying public opinion, he persuades the city to do evil things rather than good ones, what sort of fruit do you think this rhetorician would harvest from the seed he has sown?

Phaedrus: Not at all a good one.

Socrates: Don't you think, my good man, that we have chastised the art of speaking more harshly than need be? Lady Rhetoric might reply perhaps: "Astonishing fellows, what nonsense you speak. I never required anyone to be ignorant of the truth when he learns to speak, but—if my counsel means something—to master the truth and then take me up. But I do make one major claim: without me, in no way will a man who knows the truth be able to persuade with art."

Phaedrus: Will she not be just when saying this?

Socrates: Yes, I would say so, provided that the arguments assailing her testify that she IS an art. For I seem to hear some arguments on the war path, as it were, bearing solemn testimony that she lies and that she IS NOT an art but an activity devoid of art. For, as the Spartans say, there can be no genuine art of speaking, either now or at any time in the future, without there being a firm hold on truth.[104]

Phaedrus: We must hear these arguments, Socrates. Lead them out so we can review what they say and how they say it.

Socrates: Approach, my noble creatures; persuade Phaedrus, this beautiful boy,[105] that unless he loves wisdom sufficiently, he will never become a competent speaker about anything. And let Phaedrus respond.

---

104 It is likely that *etymos* is used here to recall Stesichorus' and Socrates' previous palinodes in this dialogue (see note 59). For the argument that rhetoric is artless, also see Plato's *Gorgias* 462b-c.

105 See Glossary under *Beloved*. "This beautiful boy" is a literal translation of *kallipaida* and echoes Socrates' address of the boy to whom he delivers the

Phaedrus: Ask away.

Socrates: Isn't the art of rhetoric, taken as a whole, a certain guiding of souls[106] through words, not only in the law courts and other places of public assembly but also in private? Doesn't the same art deal with major and minor matters and is it any more honorable, if correctly employed, when used in serious matters than when used in trivial ones? Or how have you heard these things?   **b**

Phaedrus: No, by god, not at all in the way you've described it. The art of rhetoric in speech or written form is most evident in the courts, also in the public assembly in speech form. I have not heard the term applied more widely.

Socrates: Why is that? Do you mean that you have only heard of Nestor's rhetorical treatises, or Odysseus', which they wrote in their idle moments at Troy, but nothing of Palamedes' treatise?[107]

---

palinode (cf. 243e); an ancient source argues that here the word means "a father of beautiful offspring," that is, a begetter of speeches (for which, see 242a-b). In either case, Socrates is punning on Phaedrus' name: *kallipaida te Phaidron*. The words "sufficiently" and "competent" translate *hikanos* (the adverbial form) and *hikanos* (the adjectival form).

[106] There are two key and shocking aspects of this definition of rhetoric. The first regards the term "a certain guiding of souls" (*psychagogia tis*), a word with a negative connotation at this time, suggesting for the dead a conjuring up of souls from the underworld (as in Aristophanes' *Birds* 1555) and for the living persuasion through witchcraft or enchantment. See Plato's *Laws* 909b when criticizing certain Sophists, or Isocrates, *ad Nic.* II.49; cf. Aristotle's *Poetics* 1450a33-4. The second shock for Phaedrus is the association of rhetoric with private discourse, as all handbooks discussed rhetoric only in a public context (although Lysias' and Socrates' first speech are obvious examples of rhetoric working on the private level). Socrates' definition of rhetoric here is analogous to what we find in Plato's *Gorgias*, except that there reference to soul-leading is omitted and attention is only on public persuasion, not public and private (i.e. philosophic) rhetoric (cf. 452e, 453d-54a). In this passage *psychagogia* may be used neutrally but when Socrates returns to this definition of speech and uses this word again (271c10), it cannot be doubted that he uses it in a positive sense, "the capacity of speech" (*logou dynamis*) having the potential to move the soul from the earthly realm to divine beauty. Also see note 142.

[107] The ancient Greeks show no awareness of epic oral composition. The verb here is *synegrapsaten*, used elsewhere in the dialogue for prose writing.

how rhetoric operates

c **Phaedrus**: Yes, I swear it by Zeus; I haven't heard of Nestor's either, unless you make our Gorgias a kind of Nestor and you make Odysseus a Thrasymachos or a Theodoros.[108]

Socrates: Perhaps. Let these examples pass, but tell me: what do the opposing parties do in the courts? Don't they speak on opposite sides of a case? Or what shall we say?

Phaedrus: Just that.

Socrates: About the just and the unjust?

Phaedrus: Yes.

Socrates: Isn't it the case that the person who does this with art can make
d the same argument, before the same audience, appear just at one time and, when he wants, unjust?

Phaedrus: How true.

Socrates: So in the speech in the public assembly, will he make the same argument seem good to the city at one time, and at another time its opposite?

Phaedrus: Yes, just so.

Socrates: Don't we see just this very thing in the case of the artful Palamedes from Elea so that the same things naturally seem to his listeners like and unlike, one and many, at rest and in motion?[109]

Phaedrus: That's certainly true.

---

[108] In Homer, men could exhibit excellence (*arete*) on the battlefield or in public speaking in the *agora*; Nestor and Odysseus were renowned especially for their ability to persuade others. Palamedes, who was part of the Trojan expedition but almost unmentioned in Homeric epic, was famous for his cunning (and in some traditions, though not in the *Phaedrus*, credited with inventing the Greek alphabet). In Athens' democracy, where all citizens were theoretically on equal footing, the art of public speaking was particularly praised. Athenians enjoyed comparing contemporary speakers to Homeric heroes. It is significant that none of the contemporary speakers singled out here are Athenian citizens, although the Athenians were considered masters of rhetoric. All three may have taught rhetoric in Athens. Gorgias, the most skillful of the three, is from Leontini in Sicily; Thrasymachos comes from Chalcedon in the north and plays a major role in Book I of the *Republic* (and is mentioned later in this dialogue at 267c); the now-forgotten Theodorus is from Byzantium and is credited with writing a handbook on rhetoric (cf. 266e).

[109] The Palamedes from Elea (in Sicily) is Zeno, famous for his paradoxes, especially one about a racer gaining on his opponent by cutting the gap in halves and never surpassing him. He is also famous for demonstrating how an opponent's argument leads to separate and contradictory conclusions. Perhaps in this context, Socrates groups him among the sophists.

Socrates: So, there is argument and counter-argument not only in the courts and places of public assembly but it seems that in all cases of speaking there would be one and the same art of some kind (if indeed it is an art) which enables someone to make everything similar to everything else, provided that things are comparable and able to be compared and, when someone else makes these similarities but hides the fact that he is doing so, to bring this to light. **e**

Phaedrus: What sort of similarities do you mean?

Socrates: It will become clear, I think, if we ask the question in this way: is deception more likely to exist when the difference between things is great or small?

Phaedrus: When the difference is small. **262a**

Socrates: And when you go from one thing to its opposite, surely you will escape notice more easily if you take small steps rather than large ones.

Phaedrus: How could it be otherwise?

Socrates: So, if one intends to deceive someone else and not be deceived himself, he must discern accurately the similarities and dissimilarities of things.

Phaedrus: Yes; that's imperative.

Socrates: Can anyone who does not know the truth in each case possibly distinguish the similarities great and small between something he doesn't know and other things?

Phaedrus: Impossible. **b**

Socrates: For people who hold opinions contrary to the things themselves and are deceived, it is clear that this deception slips in through certain likenesses.

Phaedrus: Yes, it happens in just this way.

Socrates: Will it be possible, then, for a man with art to lead anyone incrementally, step by small step, through similarities away from the truth to its opposite (and avoid being deceived himself), if he is not knowledgeable in each case of the things that are?

Phaedrus: No, never.

Socrates: Therefore, my comrade, someone who does not know the truth but has hunted down public opinion will exhibit an art of speech which is at once laughable in some way, as it seems, and artless. **c**

Phaedrus: Probably.

Socrates: So in Lysias' speech which you have in your hand now and in our speeches, would you like to consider what we said with, and without, art?

Phaedrus: I'd like nothing more, especially as we are not offering sufficient examples and our present speech is somehow bare.

d **Socrates**: All right, then. By some chance, as it seems, both the speeches were models of sorts, revealing how someone who knows the truth could play around with words and lead his audience on. And, Phaedrus, I consider that the gods of this place are the cause of this, and maybe the prophets of the Muses, as well, the ones singing over our heads who might have breathed this gift of honor into us.[110] At any rate, I have no share in any art of speaking, I suspect.

Phaedrus: Let it be as you say. Only make your words clear.

Socrates: Come on, read the beginning of Lysias' speech.

e **Phaedrus**: "You understand my affairs, and you've already heard how I think they help us both, when things work out. Nor do I expect to fail to get what I ask for just because I don't happen to be in love with you. When lovers lose their passion, they come to regret..."

Socrates: Stop. Our job is to note where he errs and what he makes without art, isn't it?

263a **Phaedrus**: Yes.

Socrates: Isn't this much clear to all—that, generally speaking, we agree about some words,[111] but are divided over others?

Phaedrus: I think I know what you mean, but still, try to speak more clearly.

Socrates: When someone says "iron" or "silver," don't we all think of the same thing?

Phaedrus: Certainly.

Socrates: But how about when we say "just" or "good"? Do some interpret them in one way, and others in another way, and don't we part company both with each other—and with ourselves?

Phaedrus: Absolutely.

b **Socrates**: In some things, then, we agree; in others, not.

Phaedrus: Right.

---

[110] There is some dispute about what two speeches Socrates is referring to. Most understand the reference to include Lysias' speech and Socrates' two speeches counted as one. But as Lysias' speech could not have been inspired by the cicadas, it seems more likely that the two speeches refer only to Socrates' two. "Lead on" (*parago*) is usually translated "mislead" but the more neutral "lead on" or "influence" fits the context better. The word is also used in a neutral sense at 261a2, its only other appearance in the dialogue. "The gods are the cause" could also be translated "I blame the gods"; again context suggests the more neutral reading. For the gods "in this place," see notes 18, 113, and 117.

[111] The text is far from clear here; I follow Richards' emendation, taking "words" for "such things."

Socrates: In which, then, are we more easily deceived, and in which is rhetoric more powerful?

Phaedrus: Clearly in those cases when we flounder about.

Socrates: Then, anyone interested in pursuing rhetorical art must first of all divide these words systematically and grasp some defining characteristics of these two forms of words, distinguishing which words will necessarily cause the most people to flounder about and which will not.

Phaedrus: He who grasps this would have really understood a beautiful c
thing—no question about that.

Socrates: Second, I take it, that as a rhetorician approaches each *word*[112] it has not escaped his notice but he observes sharply whether what he is about to say belongs to one of these classes or the other.

Phaedrus: Yes, and so?

Socrates: What then? Regarding love, shall we say that it belongs to the class of disputed words, or not?

Phaedrus: The disputed class, without a doubt. Or do you think it would have been possible for you to say what you did about it just now, that love is harmful both to the beloved and the lover, and again that it is the greatest of good things?

Socrates: Very well said. But tell me this also—for I can't entirely remem- d
ber because a god possessed me. Did I define love at the beginning of my speech?[113]

Phaedrus: Yes, by god, you did, absolutely yes.

Socrates: Ah! So you claim that the Nymphs, the daughters of Achelous, and Pan, Hermes' son,[114] are much more artful in making speeches than is Lysias, the son of Kephalos! Or is this nonsense, and did Lysias too, at the beginning of his erotic speech, compel us to see Eros as one definite thing (the way he wanted us to see him) and did he then pro- e
ceed to the end of his speech, arranging everything in order to this perception? Would you like to read the beginning of that speech again?

---

[112] The Greek does not specify the noun to which "each" refers. Following Richards' emendation, the referent would be "words."

[113] As at 262d, it is not clear to what this refers. Socrates defines love at the beginning of the first speech (237c-238c) but in the second speech only defines love after he has discussed the four forms of divine madness (252bc; cf. 249c). The singular here for speech may refer to both speeches as one, or more likely only to the first speech, as only in that speech does a definition come at the beginning of the speech.

[114] Socrates ends the dialogue with a prayer to Pan (279b), a god who almost never appears in other Platonic writings. In Plato's *Cratylus*, Socrates describes Pan with a goat-like and rough lower body and a human and smooth upper body; he is also associated with speech.

Phaedrus: If you wish, but you won't find what you're looking for.

Socrates: Read, so I can hear how he does it.

264a
Phaedrus: "You understand my affairs, and you've already heard how I think they help us both, when things work out. Nor do I expect to fail to get what I ask for just because I don't happen to be in love with you.

When lovers lose their passion, they come to regret whatever benefits they may have conferred."

Socrates: He's really far from doing what we're looking for, it appears. He doesn't start at the beginning, but at the end, swimming through the speech upstream on his back, beginning with what a lover would say to his darling after his love is gone. Or is this nonsense, Phaedrus, dear heart?[115]

b **Phaedrus**: It is to be sure, Socrates, an end, and he makes his speech about that.

Socrates: And what about the rest? Doesn't it seem as if the elements in the speech were poured out in a heap? Or would you say that what came second must by some necessity come second or that any part had to come where it does? It seemed to me in my ignorance that he said, not without some nobility, whatever came to mind as he wrote. Did you find any compelling logic of composition by which he arranged one thought after another systematically?

c **Phaedrus**: You're kind to think that I'm able to make such a critical assessment of his work.

Socrates: But I suspect that you would say this at least: every speech like a living creature should be put together with its own body so that it is not without a head or without a foot but has a middle and extremities, written in such a way that its parts fit together and form a whole.

Phaedrus: How could it be otherwise?

Socrates: Consider, then, whether your comrade's speech is composed like a living creature or not, and you will find that it differs not at all from the epigram which some say was inscribed on the tomb of Midas, the old king of Phrygia.

d **Phaedrus**: What sort of epigram is that and what's wrong with it?

Socrates: It reads like this:

> A bronze maiden I am; on Midas' remains I lie.
> So long as rain falls and mighty oaks grow,
> Stationed here by this much-lamented tomb,
> I announce to travelers-by that Midas is buried here.

---

[115] "Dear heart," literally "dear head," an expression of endearment found in epic (cf. *Il.* 8.281); cf. Socrates' reference to Phaedrus as "divine head" (234d).

You can see, I think, that it hardly matters in what order you read these   e
lines.

Phaedrus: Socrates, you're scoffing at our speech!

Socrates: Then, let's drop it lest you be upset. Yet, it seems to me that
Lysias' speech does offer abundant examples which could be profit-
ably examined, provided no one attempted to imitate them—but let's
go on to our other speeches, for in them, I think, there was something
useful to look at for those interested in examining speeches.

Phaedrus: What would that be?   265a

Socrates: The two were opposites; one said that the lover should be favored; the other the non-lover.

Phaedrus: Yes, and in a very manly manner, too.

Socrates: I thought you would speak the truth and say "in a mad manner." That is what I was looking for. We said that love was a kind of
madness. Didn't we?

Phaedrus: Yes.

Socrates: And that there were two forms of madness, one caused by human illness, the other by a divine upheaval of customary beliefs.

Phaedrus: Yes, exactly.   b

Socrates: Of the divine type, we separated out four parts assigned to four
gods: a seer's inspiration coming from Apollo, mystical initiation ascribed to Dionysos, a poetic madness coming from the Muses, and a
fourth madness coming from Aphrodite and Eros (Love) which we
called an erotic madness and the best. In some way, though I can't say
exactly how, we offered an image of erotic experience and perhaps
touched upon a truth in some instances and in others were wide of
the mark, blending together a not totally unpersuasive account in a   c
playful way—but also in a measured way and with due reverence—in
a mythic hymn to your master and mine, Phaedrus, to Eros, the guardian of beautiful boys.[116]

---

[116] The verb *prospaizo* has two meanings: "to do something in a playful manner" (as at 262d2) and "to sing in praise of." Both meanings apply to the
hymn of the palinode (cf. 247c3-4), characterized as playful speech at 262d2,
as the dialogue is characterized at 278b7 (where it is also characterized as
"measured speech," as is the hymn to Pan at the end of the dialogue (279c)).
Benardete comments that the nature of Socratic play is somehow related to
the cultic meaning of the verb, that is, playfulness in speech is a response to
the gulf that separates divine and human *logoi* (259d). When one approaches
the divine in cult, *prospaizei* refers to cultic song and dance and when one
approaches the divine in speech, *prospaizei* refers to praise (i.e. nothing to
do with irony) and to performance (as in actors addressing an audience).

Phaedrus: And, for me, certainly not unpleasant to the ear.

Socrates: Then, let's take up what follows from this point: how was the speech able to pass from censure to praise.[117]

Phaedrus: What do you have in mind?

Socrates: I'd say that everything else was in fact done in play for sport, but that some things were mentioned by chance and two of these hit upon forms or aspects[118] of speech which would not be unpleasant to

d   seize upon if someone had the power to capture their power by means of a systematic art.

Phaedrus: What things?

Socrates: The first involves someone whose sight can bring into a single form things which have previously been scattered in all directions so that by defining each thing he makes clear any subject he ever wants to teach about. So just now speaking about Eros, we defined what it is, whether well or poorly. The definition, at least, allowed the speech to progress with clarity and internal consistency.

Phaedrus: And what do you say the second form is, Socrates?

e   **Socrates**: To have the power, conversely, to cut up a composition, form by form according to its natural joints and not to try to hack through any part as a bad butcher might. Rather take the example of the two recent speeches which seized upon one common form to explain the loss of

266a   coherent thought; just as the body, which is one thing, is naturally divided into pairs of things with both parts having the same name (called, for example, left arm and right arm), so also the two speeches assumed that madness is by its nature one form in us, though capable of being divided into two parts. One of the speeches cut the part on the left and did not cease cutting until it found among these parts something called "left love" and then, with absolute justice, abused it; the other speech, however, led us to the madness on the right side and discovered there a love with the same name as the other but of some

b   divine nature. Setting this before us, the speech praised it as the greatest cause of good for us.

Phaedrus: This is very true.

---

[117]   Speech here refers to Socrates' two speeches. See notes 110 and 113.

[118]   Socrates uses one word, *eidea*, where I use two: "forms or aspects." I use the two words, "forms and aspects," to draw attention to the special quality of Socrates' terminology which applies the same word, *eidea*, to the eternal forms of the universe, of which the things on earth are only likenesses, or images, and to the aspects or forms of speech. As we discover in what follows, understanding the forms of the universe and the forms of speech both involve understanding the relation between the one and the many, and discovering an underlying unity out of plurality.

Socrates: I myself am certainly a lover, Phaedrus, of these processes of division and collection, so that I may have the ability to speak and think.[119] If I believe that someone else has the capacity to see into a single thing and to see the natural outgrowth from a single thing toward many things,[120] I pursue him, following "right behind in his tracks as if he were a god."[121] And furthermore—god knows whether I've been speaking correctly or not—up to now I have been calling those who have the capacity to do this, dialecticians. But tell me what we ought to call them if we follow what you and Lysias have taught us. Or is it just that art of speaking which Thrasymachos and all the others use, becoming themselves *wise*[122] at speaking and making others the same, if they are willing to bestow gifts upon their teachers as if they were kings?

c

Phaedrus: The men are kingly, although they certainly do not have the kind of knowledge that you are asking about. But you are right, I'd say, to call this form dialectical, although the rhetorical part has escaped us, I think.

Socrates: What's this? Can anything really be valuable and beautiful that is undertaken in an artful way but has omitted the dialectical method? If so, we—you and I—must not in any way dishonor such a thing and we must consider what part of the rhetorical art has been omitted.

d

---

[119] Socrates' language here is particularly dense and playful. By calling himself a lover just before he addresses Phaedrus by name, Socrates suggests, as he has repeatedly throughout the dialogue, that he's in love with Phaedrus and wishes to seduce him (i.e. philosophical pederasty and philosophy may go hand-in-hand; cf. 247c); but as it turns out, Socrates is more truly in love with the art of speech-making than with the boy in front of him. In saying that speech and thought depend upon a love of division and collection, Socrates neatly assimilates true rhetoric to dialectic, the philosopher's *mode* of discourse. The *Phaedrus*, more than any other Platonic dialogue, attempts to discover the common ground shared by these two erotic activities. This assimilation is dependent, of course, upon rhetoric's proper subordination to philosophy itself and knowledge of the truth, to the extent humanly possible. I wish to thank Frank Trivigno for elements of this formulation. (see 261aff, above, and 271c10ff, and especially 273d1ff, below).

[120] Here I follow a manuscript reading of *pephykos* modifying *hen*; many editors read *pephykota* which would translate: "to see the things which grow naturally into one thing and toward many things."

[121] Socrates appears to be adapting loosely phrasing from the *Odyssey*; see 2.406 and 5.193.

[122] See Glossary under *Art*. By calling Thrasymachos and other *sophoi*, or skilled masters of the art of speaking, Socrates implies the possible common ground between the *philo-sophos*, or lover of wisdom, and the *sophos*-rhetorician.

Phaedrus: There are a thousand such things, I suppose, Socrates, in the rhetorical textbooks.

Socrates: Good for you to remember them. First, I think, is the *prooimion*, or Preface, which must be spoken at the beginning of a speech. This is what you mean, isn't it: the refinements of the art?[123]

e **Phaedrus**: Yes.

Socrates: Second, there's the *diegesis*, or Exposition and Testimonies (*marturiai*) from witnesses for it; third, Proofs (*tekmeria*); fourth, Argument by Plausibility (*eikota*). That very good man from Byzantium, the one who is so cunning in his speeches, also mentions Confirmation (*pistosis*) and Further Confirmation (*epipistosis*), I think.

Phaedrus: Are you referring to the worthy Theodoros?

267a **Socrates**: Who else? And one must construct a Cross-Examination (*elenchon*) and a Further Cross-Examination (*epexelenchon*) in a courtroom accusation (*kategoria*) and defense (*apologia*). Shall we not bring the most elegant Euenos from Paros into our circle; he discovered Covert Allusion (*hypodelosis*) and Incidental Praise (*parepainos*). Some say that as a mnemonic device he delivered Incidental Censure (*parapsogos*) in

---

[123] Preface marks "the first item in a series of technical terms of rhetorical theory or practice which Plato amuses himself to enumerate, holding them up to ridicule," as de Vries comments *ad* 266d7. From 266d7-267e8, Socrates names 18 parts of a composition from Preface to Recapitulation, or summary (which must be arranged with a sense of the whole: 264c, 268d, 269c), and he names 10 rhetorical theorists. Not one is an Athenian citizen, but most, if not all, visited and taught in Athens: Theodorus from Byzantium (nothing more known of him); Euenos from Paros (an island in the Aegean), mentioned as a teacher in the *Apology* (20b) and a poet in the *Phaedo* (60d); Tisias of Syracuse (in Sicily), probably dead at the dramatic date of the dialogue, taught the importance of likenesses, *eikota*; Gorgias from Leontini (in Sicily), a famous sophist, his visit to Athens in 427 is seen as a landmark in the history of rhetoric; Prodicus from Ceos (an Aegean island), a sophist, a participant in Plato's *Protagoras*; Hippias from Elis (in the Peloponnese), a sophist, in Plato's *Hippias Major* and *Minor*; Polus of Acragas (in Sicily), in Plato's *Gorgias* where it is said he made rhetoric an art (462b); Likumnius from Argos or Tiryns (in the Peloponnese), said to be Gorgias' pupil, identified as a rhetorician and poet by Aristotle, *Rhetoric* III. 12, 1413b14 and 13,1414b17; Protagoras of Abdera (coast of Thrace), the most famous of the sophists, Thrasymachos of Chalcedon (opposite Byzantium), a sophist and significant figure in Plato's *Republic*. Isocrates, an Athenian and Plato's contemporary, was a student of Prodicus, Gorgias, and Tisias and boasts that he can make small things appear large and new things old (*Panegyricus* 8). "Refinements" echoes Phaedrus' characterization of Lysias' speech (227c) and the description of the grove (230c).

meter[124]—for the man is wise. Shall we let Tisias and Gorgias sleep?—men who saw that Argument by Plausibility was more valued than truths and who by the force of speech made the small appear great, and the great small; and made the newest innovations appear old, and old things new; and on all subjects discovered conciseness of speech and infinite extension. When Prodicus once heard me say this, he laughed and claimed that he alone discovered what was necessary for the art of speeches: that they be neither long nor short but of due measure.

b

Phaedrus: Most clever of you, Prodicus.

Socrates: What about Hippias? I think our friend from Elis would agree with Prodicus.

Phaedrus: Yes, and why not?

Socrates: What should we say about Polus and his Muses' Treasury of Speech, including his classifications for things like Reduplication (*diplasiologia*), Speaking in Maxims (*gnomologia*), and Speaking in Images or Similes (*eikonologia*), and those terms which Likumnius made up for him as a gift for his making of Good Diction (*euepeia*).

c

Phaedrus: Doesn't Protagoras take credit for similar inventions, Socrates?

Socrates: Yes, a certain Correct Diction (*orthoepeia*), my darling, and many other fine things. But the mighty Chalcedonian—Thrasymachos—I'd say excelled in the art of drawing out the pitiful wailings over old age and poverty.[125] He was also a clever fellow at infuriating a crowd and then with his bewitching incantations soothing the angry mob, as he put it. Also, no one was better at hurling slanders, then washing them away, whatever their source may have been. But when it comes to the end of a speech, all agree what it should be, though some call it Recapitulation (*epanodos*), while others call it something else.

d

Phaedrus: Are you referring to the summation of each point, reminding the listeners at the end of what they've heard?

Socrates: That's it, and if you have something else to add about this art...

Phaedrus: Minor points only, nothing important.

Socrates: Then let's drop them and scrutinize those other things more closely under the light and ask what in the world is the power of this art.

268a

---

[124] See Glossary under *Unskilled speaker*. *en metro* here clearly means "in verse." At 258d10, I translate as "with measured speech," while just below at 267b5 I translate *metron* as "of due measure."

[125] Socrates' phrasing parodies Thrasymachos; exaggerated rhythmical patterns of speech.

Phaedrus: A power with a very great force, Socrates, particularly when in the assemblies of the multitude.[126]

Socrates: So it is. But, my inspired fellow, also consider whether you also see holes in the fabric, as I do.

Phaedrus: Just show me.

Socrates: Tell me. If someone were to approach your friend Dr. Eruximachos or his father Dr. Akoumenos and proclaim: "I know how to apply certain things to a body to make it warm, or to cool it down, as I wish, and I know how to induce vomiting, if need be, or in turn to make the body emit from the other end, and everything else of this kind. With this knowledge I consider myself worthy to be a doctor and to make someone else a doctor by passing along this knowledge to him." What do you think they would say, hearing this?

b

Phaedrus: How else but to ask if he also knew who needed these treatments, and when, and for how long?

Socrates: If he should reply: "I know none of these things, but I judge that my student learning from me will be able on his own to practice what you ask about."

c

Phaedrus: I think they would say that he was a raving madman, if he thinks he has become a doctor after hearing something from a book or happening upon a few drugs, when he has no understanding of the art.

Socrates: What if someone were to approach Sophocles or Euripides and say that he knew how to make very long speeches about small things and very short ones about great things, and to compose pitiful laments at will or, by contrast, threats and scares, and such things, and that teaching these things he knows how to transmit the making of tragedy?

d

Phaedrus: I suspect, they would also laugh, Socrates, if someone thinks that tragedy is anything less than the proper arrangement of parts, each fitted appropriately in relation to the other and to the whole.

Socrates: But I don't think that they would revile them harshly but speak the way a musician might if he came upon a man who thought that he understood harmony when he simply happened to know how to

---

[126] It is difficult to determine whether Phaedrus is critical or admiring of this power: his language clearly refers to Athens' democracy and in less than a flattering light: assemblies translates *synodoi* which can refer to public gatherings in assemblies or political unions. Plato often uses *plethos* (a great number, multitude, mob) as a stand in for *demos*, the political body of Athens. Regardless of tone, Phaedrus still thinks of rhetoric in terms of public speech, despites Socrates' efforts to refine rhetoric as an art in private as well as in public settings (261a-b).

make the highest and lowest note. He wouldn't bark out: "You're sick,   e
crazy in the head," but because he's musical he'd say more gently: "My
excellent man, while it is necessary to know these things if one intends
to understand the laws of harmony, it's quite possible that a man with
your level of expertise might not know the slightest thing about harmony. You see, you know the prerequisites for harmony but not har-
monics itself."

Phaedrus: How perfectly true.

Socrates: So too Sophocles would say that his man was displaying to them   269a
the prerequisites for tragedy but not the tragic art; and Dr. Akoumenos
similarly that his man knew the prerequisites for healing but not the
healing art.

Phaedrus: Just so.

Socrates: What do you think the honey-tongued Adrastos, or even Pericles,
would say if they should hear about these absolutely beautiful techniques
we've been discussing—Speaking Concisely and Similes and the other
such things which we were going through and scrutinizing under the
light. Like you and me, would they bark at them and utter some igno-   b
rant phrase against those who wrote and taught these things as if they
were a rhetorical art; or, because they are more skillful than we are, would
they actually chastise us, saying: "Phaedrus and Socrates, you shouldn't
be harsh but forgiving if some people don't know how to think dialectically and are unable therefore to define what rhetoric is. On this account, they think that they have discovered the rhetorical art when they   c
know only its prerequisites; and teaching others these things they believe that they have taught the art perfectly and that their students themselves must on their own come up with a way of saying each of the
parts persuasively and with a way of fitting the parts appropriately into
the whole, thinking that this is no work at all."[127]

Phaedrus: But surely, Socrates, the art which these men teach and write
about as rhetoric in their handbooks is something like this. What you've
said is true, I think. But the real art of rhetoric and persuasion, how   d
and from what source can one come by this?

Socrates: If you mean the ability, Phaedrus, to become a perfect competi-
tor, it is probably—I'd say certainly—just like everything else. If you
have an innate ability for rhetoric, you'll become a famous rhetorician,
provided that you acquire knowledge and work at your art; but if your
natural abilities fall short of this, you'll be less than perfect. But to the
extent that there is art in this whole business, you're not likely to find
the method or right approach, I'd say, where Lysias or Thrasymachos
go.

---

[127] The arrangement of Socrates' own sentence progressively degenerates, no
doubt to illustrate humorously the importance of his point.

Phaedrus: But where, then?

e **Socrates**: My excellent friend, in all likelihood Pericles is the most perfect of all the Greeks in this art.

Phaedrus: How so?

270a **Socrates**: All of the great arts are in need of highfalutin prattling and star-gazin theorizing about nature. For this kind of lofty thought and working through to perfection in every way seems somehow to enter in from that source. And Pericles achieved this, topping off his natural talent. Falling in with a man like Anaxagoras and being filled with star-gazin theorizing and coming to understand the nature of mind and mindlessness – the very things Anaxagoras discussed at great length, Pericles drew from all this and applied what fit to the art of speech.[128]

Phaedrus: Explain what you mean.

b **Socrates**: That the medical art works in the same way as the rhetorical art, I suppose.

Phaedrus: How so?

Socrates: In both you need to determine its nature, of the body in one, of the soul in the other, if you intend (not merely with empirical practice but with art) to instill health and strength by applying drugs and diet for one, and to impart excellence and the persuasion you wish by applying words and customary rules of conduct for the other.[129]

Phaedrus: This seems plausible enough, Socrates.

c **Socrates**: Do you think that it is possible to understand the nature of the soul at all intelligently without understanding the nature of the whole?[130]

Phaedrus: If we are to follow Hippocrates at all, Ascelpius' heir, it is not possible to understand anything about the body either without this method.

---

[128] Socrates is certainly speaking ironically about Pericles and Anaxagoras' good influence upon him. In Plato's *Gorgias* (503c, 515c-16d), he has a low opinion of Pericles' rhetoric, nor in the *Apology* (26d-e) does he feel much affinity for Anaxagoras' work. In the *Clouds*, Aristophanes mocks Socrates' usage. By contrast, Plutarch in his *Life of Pericles* (4-6 and 8) reads Socrates' praise of Pericles as genuine. See Philip Slater, *A Commentary on Plutarch's Pericles* (Chapel Hill, 1989) 77.

[129] By contrast, divine erotic madness causes an upheaval of customary beliefs (265a).

[130] Socrates does not specify the whole of what. He is referring most likely to the nature of the whole universe; the other possibility is the nature of the whole human being (i.e. body and soul). See also 270cd.

Socrates: He speaks well, my friend, but it's still necessary, Hippocrates aside, to examine this account and ask whether it squares with ours.

Phaedrus: I agree.

Socrates: Consider, then, how Hippocrates and the true account speak about the nature of something. This is how we should speak about the nature of anything whatsoever: first, we should ask whether a nature is simple or multi-formed in regard to which we wish to be artful and to be able to make others artful. Then, if simple, we should consider its natural capacity, that is, what it can do to what, or in what ways it can be acted upon and by what. If it has multiple forms, we must count these and examine each of them as we did when we looked at the simple form: what is its natural capacity to do what to what or to suffer what by what.   **d**

Phaedrus: Possibly, Socrates.

Socrates: At any rate to approach the subject without asking other questions would be like traveling with a blind man. On the other hand, whoever pursues anything with art must never be compared to the blind or deaf. Rather, it is clear that if someone teaches another how to make speeches with art, he will demonstrate precisely the essence of the nature of that to which the speeches are applied.[131] And that, doubtless, will be the soul.   **e**

Phaedrus: Surely.

Socrates: Then all the efforts of this man are concentrated on this. For it's persuasion which he tries to implant in the soul. Doesn't he?   **271a**

Phaedrus: Yes.

Socrates: It is clear, then, that Thrasymachos, and whoever else seriously teaches the art of rhetoric, will first describe the soul with full precision and make us see whether she is one and homogenous by nature or multi-formed like the figure of the body, since, as we said, this is what it means to demonstrate the nature of something.

Phaedrus: Yes, absolutely.

Socrates: Secondly, he will reveal what it naturally does to what or what it naturally suffers from what.

Phaedrus: Yes, surely.

Socrates: Thirdly, having classified the different kinds of speeches and kinds of soul and how these are affected, he will go through every cause,   **b**

---

131   At the beginning of the discussion about rhetoric, Phaedrus used the phrase *tekhne legein* to refer to those who speak with art in public places like the law courts (261b). Socrates has turned the argument so that now it refers to those who reveal the essential nature of the thing described.

aligning each type of speech to each type of soul, explaining the rea- son why one soul is necessarily persuaded by speeches of a certain sort and another is not.[132]

Phaedrus: This certainly would be the best way, in all likelihood.

Socrates: There is, my friend, no other way than this. If a model of a speech or an actual speech were made in some other way, it would never be
c   spoken or written with art. But the writers today who produce Speech Manuals[133] (things you have heard) are rogues and keep the nature of the soul hidden from view, although they have a perfectly beautiful understanding of it. But until they speak and write in this way, let us not believe that they write with knowledge of this art.

Phaedrus: What way is that?

Socrates: It is not easy to offer the exact words but I am willing to say how one must write if one intends to be as artful as possible.

Phaedrus: Go on, then.

d   **Socrates:** Since the capacity of speech is to guide the soul, someone in- tending to become a rhetorician must know what forms the soul pos- sesses.[134] The number of forms is so and so; their quality such and such; hence some people are of this sort and others of that sort. When these divisions are made, he needs again to know that the forms of speeches are so and so and the quality of each such and such. Therefore, people of this sort can be easily persuaded by such and such for this or that reason to do one thing or another, while people of a different sort are

---

[132]   Socrates appears to have in mind a complex soul of multiple parts, more diverse and complex, it would seem, than the tripartite soul of appetite, courage, and reason outlined in the *Republic*. "Different kinds of soul" trans- lates *ta...psyches gene*. At 271d1-2, Socrates varies the expression, saying *psyche hosa eide echei* ("what forms the soul possesses"), phrases which I treat as roughly synonymous. Some argue that *gene* (in the first phrase) should be translated as "parts" and *eide* (in the second) as "kinds," but this distinc- tion seems forced. At 270d1 and 271a7, the word for a multi-formed soul is *polyeidos*, perhaps analogous to *polyplokoteron*, polymorphic used to describe some mythic, mixed-bodied beasts at 230a4. *Polyeides* is also used to de- scribe many-limbed excess (following the manuscript reading) at 238a3. At 277c2-3, Socrates draws a further distinction between a dappled, many-col- ored (*poikile*) and a simple (*haple*) soul. Socrates uses the same adjective *haple* (at 230a5-6) to contrast tamer, simpler beings with a share of divinity in them from wilder, polymorphic creatures. Also see notes 35, 46, and 155.

[133]   At 266ff, Socrates discusses a number of these manuals. When Socrates says that these present-day writers have a complete and thorough knowledge of the soul, he is being ironic, of course.

[134]   See notes 2 and 131.

hard to persuade for these reasons. The aspiring rhetorician must think these matters through in a sufficient manner and then, after that, observing them in actuality and being lived out before his eyes, he must be able to trace these actions keenly and perceptively, or else he won't be any better off than he was when he was absorbing these words in school. Only when he is able to explain sufficiently what type of person is persuaded by what type of speech and he has the ability to perceive and to determine for himself in the case of an individual he meets that he is this type of person and his nature is the very type that he heard about in school, and now that he finds himself in front of this man, he must apply these particular words in that particular way to persuade him of these things. After the young rhetorician has mastered all this and understood the appropriate times – both opportune and inopportune—for speaking and for holding back, for concise speech, for speech which stirs pity, for exaggeration, and for each of the other forms of speech he has learnt, only then, and not before, has the art been beautifully and perfectly mastered. But whenever in speaking, teaching, or writing he falls short in these matters but claims that he speaks with art, then the person who does not believe him is the stronger. "What do you think?" the prose-writer of this treatise might say. "Is it like this, Phaedrus and Socrates, or must the art of speaking be described differently?"

Phaedrus: It is not possible to describe it otherwise, Socrates, I suppose. Yet, this seems to be no small undertaking.

Socrates: True enough. That's why we must turn all the arguments every which way to consider whether there isn't an easier and more concise road to this art, so as not to go off on a long and rough path in vain when there is a short and smooth one available. And if from your listening to Lysias or anyone else you have any tips, try to remember them and tell us.

Phaedrus: I could try, but now I have nothing to say.

Socrates: Then, may I put in a word which I heard from some of those concerned about these things?

Phaedrus: Yes, surely.

Socrates: We hear after all, Phaedrus, that it's fair to hear the wolf's side of the story, too.

Phaedrus: And so, go on.

Socrates: Well now, they say there's no need to revere these matters so or to climb such a long and circuitous path. For in every way—just as we said at the beginning of this speech[135]—if you want to become a

---

[135] Cf. 259e.

satisfactory orator there's no need to know the truth about good and just deeds or even whether human beings are this way or that by nature or by up-bringing. People in the courts couldn't give a fig for the truth about such matters, only for what is persuasive. The Plausible Argument, that's what you must turn to, if you want to speak with art. Sometimes it's imperative not even to mention what really happened, if it wasn't plausible enough; replace it with plausible arguments whether in a prosecution or a defense. Always be in pursuit of the Plausibility and bid the truth a hearty farewell. Stick to this throughout the entire speech and you've got the sum total of the art.

Socrates is Saying its OK to LIE?!

273a

e

Phaedrus: You've described perfectly, Socrates, what these self-professing speech artists claim. For I recall that we touched on this sort of thing briefly before and this seems to be the all-important point for people concerned with these matters.

Socrates: And I'm sure you've tramped through Tisias' work carefully. So let him tell us about this too: does he say that the Plausible Argument is anything other than the opinion of the masses?

b

Phaedrus: How could it be otherwise?

Socrates: Apparently having discovered this wise—and artful—technique, Tisias wrote that if a weak but brave man clobbers a strong but cowardly man and steals his cloak or something and is then dragged into court, it is imperative that neither man tell the truth. The coward must deny that he was clobbered by the brave man alone, and the defendant must establish through cross-examination that the two were alone, and make full use of that old saw: "How could a man like me lay a finger on a man like him?" The poor plaintiff will never admit his own cowardice but would try to make up another lie, quickly handing over a second opportunity for his adversary to cross examine. So in other scenarios as well, the rules of the art are like this. Aren't they, Phaedrus?

c

Phaedrus: Yes, surely.

Socrates: I'll be! What a cleverly concealed art, it seems, Tisias has unearthed, or whoever it may have been and whatever is the name which pleases him.[136] But, comrade, should we or shouldn't we say to him—

Phaedrus: Say what?

d

Socrates: This: "Tisias, before you even appeared we had been saying for some time that most people hit upon this plausibility thing because it resembles the truth; we had just now explained how in every instance the man who knows the truth understands most beautifully how to find

---

[136] Socrates, presumably, is referring to Corax (The Crow) of Syracuse (5th century), an obscure figure who is said to be the first teacher of rhetoric and Tisias' teacher. But it is equally possible that Corax is Tisias' nickname. See note 123.

these resemblances. Consequently, if you have something different to say about the art of speeches, we would listen; but if not, we shall be persuaded by what we have just explained, namely that, unless someone both enumerates the natures of those who are about to listen and is able to divide up beings according to their forms and to comprehend each individual thing by its unique form, he will not be an artist of speeches (to the extent that any human being can be). Nor will he ever acquire these skills without much diligence. A moderate man does not put himself through this labor in order to speak and to act in the company of human beings, but to put himself in a position to say what is gratifying to the gods and at all times to act in a gratifying manner to the best of his ability.[137] For certainly, Tisias, men wiser than we say that a man of intelligence must not concern himself with gratifying fellow slaves, except in a secondary way, but rather with gratifying masters who are good and from good stock.[138] So, if the circuit is long, don't be astonished. For great things – distinct from the goals you set— one must take the long way around. And yet, as our speech says, even these successes, should one wish them, best come from those more circuitous pursuits.

e

274a

Phaedrus: That's said very beautifully, it seems to me, Socrates, if only anyone could do it.

Socrates: And yet even in reaching for the beautiful there is beauty, and also in suffering whatever it is that one suffers en route.

b

Phaedrus: Certainly.   \ the process is important/significant too

Socrates: Let this then be enough about the art and artlessness of speeches.[139]

Phaedrus: Yes, surely.

Socrates: But it remains to consider, doesn't it, what's befitting and what's not fitting in writing; when it is done well and when it's not fitting?[140]

---

137 Note the lexical shift: the verb used here to describe human gratification of the gods through speech is the same which was used from the beginning of the dialogue by Phaedrus, Lysias, and Socrates to describe the favors which the beloved should grant to the lover (or non-lover).

138 For "from good stock," compare 246a8 in reference to the white horse of the soul. Some argue that this phrase cannot apply to gods and must be understood figuratively as meaning "wholly good." But in the context of slaves and masters, the notion of good stock, as well as good habits, is not out of place. Furthermore, in Greek mythology, if not in Plato, gods can be bad and behave badly.

139 This concludes a definition which begins at 271c6. For a concise summary, see 277b4-c6 and note 152. Socrates never explains under what circumstances one form of rhetoric or another should be practiced.

140 The question was first posed at 257d.

Phaedrus: Yes.

Socrates: Do you know how best to gratify god in the matter of speeches, whether in the making of them or in the delivery?

Phaedrus: I have no idea. Do you?

c **Socrates**: I can report what I heard from our ancestors but only they know the truth of it. If we should discover this ourselves, would any of these mortal speculations concern us?

Phaedrus: That's a silly question. But tell me what you say you've heard.

Socrates: Well now, I heard[141] that near Naucratis in Egypt there was one of the ancient gods whose sacred bird they call Ibis. The name of this divinity was Theuth.[142] He was the first to discover number and calcu-
d lation, as well as geometry and astronomy, besides the games of draughts and dice, but especially he invented letters. At that time the king of all Egypt was Thamus who reigned from the great city of the Upper Kingdom[143] which the Greeks call Egyptian Thebes, and Thamus they call the god Ammon.[144] Coming to Thamus, Theuth showed all his arts and said that they must be distributed to the rest of the Egyptians, but Thamus asked what benefit there might be in each art. After
e Theuth explained the merits of each, Thamus censured some and

---

[141] At 275b3-4, Phaedrus will imply that Socrates has made up this story. While the story echoes the conflict between Zeus and Prometheus regarding the Titan's gift of fire and many arts (*tekhnai*), including the invention of writing, to humans, it does so in the context of Egyptian and Greek mythological elements. Many Greeks admired the Egyptians for their wisdom, technological skills, and ability to trace their history back over many generations (cf. Herodotus 2.77); so in Plato's *Timaeus*, an Egyptian priest recounts the ancient myth of Atlantis. In Plato's *Philebus*, Thoth is involved with another story about the alphabet, one among the many, diverse myths the Greeks had about the origins of writing. Naucratis was a Greek trading colony.

[142] Theuth (or Thoth) is the Egyptian god of writing, numbers, and geometry, and is represented as an ibis. The Greeks associated him with Hermes, no doubt because both were associated with weighing and leading souls. Hermes' role as *psychopomp*, "leader of souls," is analogous with Socrates' definition of rhetoric as *psychogogia*, "guiding souls." See 261a8 and 271c10, and note 106.

[143] Upper Kingdom, *tou ano topos*, perhaps punning on "upper place."

[144] The Egyptians believed in god-kings. I accept Postgate's emendation of *thamoun* (Thamus) for *theon* ("god"). According to Herodotus (2.42), Ammon, also known as the sun god Ra, is the Egyptian name for Zeus; This god-king differs from a philosopher-king in that he pronounces, more in the manner of a prophet (cf. 275c8), than of a philosopher exploring the truth of a statement.

praised others, depending upon whether Theuth seemed to speak beautifully or not.[145]

The story goes that Thamus said many things to Theuth about each art—both pro and con—the details of which would take too long to go through. When speaking about letters, Theuth said: "This branch of learning, my king, will make the Egyptians wiser and will improve their memory. The drug[146] for memory and wisdom has been discovered!"—to which the king responded: "Oh, Theuth, the greatest of technicians,[147] one person is granted the ability to beget the things of art, another the ability to judge what measure of harm and benefit they hold for those who intend to use them. And now you, father of these letters, have in your fondness for them said what is the opposite of their real effect. For this will produce a forgetting in the souls of those who learn these letters as they fail to exercise their memory, because those who put trust in writing recollect from the outside with foreign signs, rather than themselves recollecting from within by themselves. You have not discovered a drug for memory, but for reminding.[148] You offer your students an apparent, not a true wisdom. For they have heard much from you without real teaching, and they will appear rich in knowledge when for the most part there's an absence of knowledge, and they will be difficult to be with since they appear wise rather than really being wise."

Phaedrus: Socrates, how easily you construct stories about Egypt or any other place you want.

Socrates: But, my friend, those at Zeus' sanctuary in Dodona claim that the speeches of oak trees were the first prophetic words. Because people back then weren't wise the way you young are today, it was enough

---

[145] For speaking well (*kalos*), also see 274b7. According to this argument, to speak well means to speak with an understanding of the true nature of the thing discussed.

[146] Greeks were particularly sensitive to the fact that a *pharmakon*, "drug," could have a positive or negative effect. Frequently, Greeks said that drugs came from Egypt. For other occurences of this word in the dialogue, see note 19. Writing as a "drug against forgetfulness" is already found in a fragment of a play by Euripides, the *Palamedes*, a figure who like Theuth is an inventor of writing, numbers, draughts and dice. By the end of the fifth century it was a commonplace in tragedy to view writing as a drug. Cf. Nightingale, 149-54; Ferrari, 280-81.

[147] In Greek, technician derives from *tekhne*, translated throughout the dialogue as "art."

[148] Although Ammon seems to be dismissing writing as merely a reminder, Socrates uses the same word in the palinode when he says that a person who correctly handles the "reminders" of the soul's "recollection" of forms will be initiated into the perfect mysteries (cf. 249c).

c   for them in their simple-mindedness to listen to an oak or a rock so long as it spoke the truth. But perhaps it makes a difference to you who is speaking and where he comes from. Why don't you consider this alone: whether it is as they say, or not?

Phaedrus: You're right to rebuke me; about letters it does seem to be just as the Theban king says it is.

Socrates: So, the person who thinks that he is leaving behind an art in written form and the person who receives it thinking that there will be something clear and secure in these written forms would be exceedingly simple-minded and truly ignorant of Ammon's prophecy, if he

d   thinks that written speeches are anything more than reminders for a person already in the know about the things jotted down.

Phaedrus: Yes, very true.

Socrates: This is what makes writing clever and really analogous to painting, Phaedrus.[149] A painting's creations stand there as if alive, but if you question them, they remain in complete and solemn silence. The same for words written down. You might suspect that they would speak as if they understand something, but if you ask them about anything in the text in hopes of learning something, the words signify only one

e   thing, and always the same thing. And once something is written down, every speech is whirled about every which way, picked up as well by those who understand as by those who have no business reading it, a speech having no idea to whom it should speak and to whom it shouldn't. Ill-treated and unjustly abused, a speech always needs the help of its father because it is unable by itself to defend or help itself.

Phaedrus: Also, very true.

276a   Socrates: But let's consider a different kind of speech, a legitimate brother of that one, and ask how it comes into being and how it is by nature better and more capable.

Phaedrus: What is this and how do you mean that it comes into being?

Socrates: One that is written with knowledge in the soul of one who understands; this is able to defend itself and it knows when and to whom it should speak, and when and to whom it shouldn't.

Phaedrus: You are referring to the speech of the person who knows, a speech living and ensouled, the written version of which would justly be called the image.[150]

---

[149] The word for painting, zographia, literally translated means "alive or life writing"; it could also mean "animal writing."

[150] Empsykhon (also used at 245e6) literally means "having soul (or breath) in it" and is usually translated as "animate" or "breathing," but these translations obscure the link between living speech and soul. See note 55. Many

Socrates: Exactly so. And tell me this. Would a farmer with half a brain   b
sow seeds in all seriousness, if he cares for his seeds and wants them
to become fruitful, in the summer in the gardens of Adonis—you know,
in a flower box—and would he rejoice seeing them bloom beautifully
in eight days; or, whenever he did this kind of farming, would he do it
for the joy of play and Adonis' festival? But when he farms seriously
employing his art and sowing in proper soil, he would adore[151] what
he sowed when the things he planted attained perfection in the eighth
month.

Phaedrus: Yes, Socrates, he would probably do one thing seriously, the   c
other differently in the way you said.

Socrates: Shall we say that one who has knowledge of what is just, beautiful, and good is less intelligent regarding his seeds?

Phaedrus: Far from it.

Socrates: Then, he won't be serious when he writes these things in black
water,[152] sowing with a reed pen words which are incapable of defending themselves and incapable of teaching the truth adequately.

Phaedrus: No, it's not likely.

Socrates: It certainly isn't. But he sows his gardens of written words, it   d
seems, in the joy of play and he will write, whenever he does write, to
build up a treasure trove of reminders both for himself in case he
reaches forgetful old age and for all who walk down the same path,
and he'll take pleasure watching the tender shoots in the garden grow.
But when others indulge themselves in other kinds of play, finding
pleasure in drinking parties and whatever is related to these, our man,
it seems, instead of this kind of play will engage in the things I've just
mentioned.

Phaedrus: In contrast to that vulgar play, yours is very beautiful and noble,   e
Socrates, befitting a person who is able to play and make fables about
justice and the other things you speak about.[153]

Socrates: Yes, like this, my dear Phaedrus, but it is far more noble, I think,
to be serious about these things when a person uses the dialectical art

---

of the arguments and words in this sentence are also found in Alkidamas'
speech (see Appendix D): speech is alive and ensouled; written speech only
a copy, unmoving, and a painted figure. But Alkidamas does not stipulate
that a speaker know the truth about which he speaks. Compare Socrates'
comments at 275d. See note 37.

[151] See Glossary under *To Love*.

[152] I.e., ink.

[153] Cf. *mythikos hymnos* of 265c1. Phaedrus may be referring jokingly to Plato's
Republic which "makes fables" (cf. 2.378c, 382d; XX.501e) about justice. See
Glossary under *Fable*. Consider the distinction between human and divine
speech at 259d and note 102.

277a   and selects an appropriate soul, sowing and planting his speeches with knowledge, speeches which have the means to defend themselves and the one who plants them. These speeches are not fruitless but bear seed from which other speeches, planted in other fields, have the means to pass this seed on, forever immortal, and to make the person possessing them as blessed as is humanly possible.

Phaedrus: What you say is even more beautiful and noble.

Socrates: Now that we have agreed on these things, Phaedrus, we can decide the remaining questions.

Phaedrus: What are they?

Socrates: We have come to this point in the discussion to look at the following: how we should examine our criticism of Lysias for his speech b   writing and, with regard to the speeches themselves, how do we judge which ones were written with art, and which ones without. But, I'd say, we have shown with due measure what is made with art and what is not.

Phaedrus: It seemed so at the time, but remind me again, how it went.

Socrates: Until someone knows the truth about each of the things he speaks or writes about and is able to define everything according to itself and, having defined it, knows how to cut it up again according to its forms until it has come to the state where it can be cut up no more; and until that person sees thoroughly into the nature of the soul according to c   these same principles, discovering the form that most fits each nature, and accordingly makes and arranges his speech, supplying intricate or multi-colored speeches, covering all the harmonic modes for an intricate or multi-colored soul and supplying simple speech for a simple soul[154]—only then will he be able to manage the class of speeches artfully, to the degree that it is within its nature to be artful, either with respect to teaching or persuading something, as the entire earlier discussion revealed to us.[155]

---

[154] Cf. 236b7-8 where *poikilos* ("intricate, multi-colored, or dappled") also describes one kind of speech. In the *Republic*, *poilike* is used, as here, to describe the complex or intricate soul. See notes 35 and 131.

[155] This summarizes 259e1-274a5. Although rhetoric is an art dependent upon words and eros a divine madness awakened by sight, the two have much in common: they can be either multi-colored or simple, though one by nature, the other by art. Most importantly, both have the capacity to see thoroughly into the nature of souls, to select a suitable soul, and to move it, whether through rhetoric or erotic madness, towards the truth and the company of the gods. Like the divine form of eros, a proper understanding of rhetoric depends upon a true understanding of the soul and, as such, is "beneficial" for both the active agent and the recipient of that agency: i.e., for both the rhetorician and the one addressed, for the lover and beloved, at least to the extent that such art is humanly possible.

Phaedrus: This is exactly how it appeared to us.

Socrates: But regarding the question—whether it is good or shameful to   **d**
speak or write speeches, and whether it is fairly reproached or not,
didn't we just a little while ago in what we were saying make perfectly clear-

Phaedrus: What sort of thing did we make clear?

Socrates: -that we are within our rights, whether anyone else says so or
not, to reproach any writer—whether it be Lysias or someone else, who
has written or intends to write whether for private use or a public cause
when writing something political proposing laws in the belief that his
composition contains great lucidity and lasting value. Even if the entire multitude should praise it, not knowing the difference between a
waking vision and a sleeping dream[156] (when writing about justice and
injustice, or good and evil), is grounds in point of fact for reproach.   **e**

Phaedrus: It certainly is.

Socrates: But it's a different matter for a person who believes that in a
written speech on any subject there is necessarily much playfulness and
that no speech, whether written in measured speech or not, can ever
be taken too seriously—for that matter, the case is really no different
for things recited in the way that rhapsodies are delivered simply to
persuade without any thought of raising questions or offering instruction. He's aware that the best of them were really written as reminders   **278a**
for men who know, and he also believes that only what is said about
things just, beautiful and good—and these only when they are taught
and discussed for the sake of instruction and actually written in the
soul—only then can they be clear, perfect, and worthy of seriousness.
And he believes that the speeches of this sort should be regarded as
his legitimate sons, principally the sons within himself (if any is discovered therein), and secondarily any of that speech's sons and broth-   **b**
ers which have sprung up simultaneously in a worthy manner in the
souls of other men.[157] But he bids farewell to the other discourses. Such
a man, Phaedrus, is likely to be such as you and I might pray to become.

---

[156] The distinction between a waking vision (*hypar*) and a sleeping dream (*onar*)
here may be parallel to the earlier distinction (at 276a8-9) between a speech
which is living and filled with soul and a written composition which is an
image (*eidolon*) of it. See note 150.

[157] Hackforth on this passage: "A man's legitimate spiritual children are primarily those truths which he himself has discovered by a process of dialectic,
and secondarily those which, while logically consequent upon the former,
are actually reached, again dialectically, by others. The distinction no doubt
reflects the relation between the head of a school (such as Plato himself)
and its members or disciples building upon his teaching." For "composed in
measured speech" above, see note 37.

Phaedrus: In every way possible, I hope and pray for what you are saying.[158]

Socrates: So then, let's say that we have played out our discussion of speeches with due measure.[159] Now go and inform Lysias that we have gone down to the spring of the Nymphs and the shrine of the Muses

c   and heard speeches which commanded that we inform Lysias and anyone else arranging[160] speeches, and Homer also and anyone else who has arranged poetry with or without the accompaniment of music, and thirdly that we inform Solon and anyone else who has in political speeches written tracts that he calls laws: if a person has arranged these pieces knowing wherein the real truth lies; and if he is able to defend them when submitting his writings to cross-examination; and if he can when speaking expose the trivialities of written things, then such a person should not have a name which derives from

d   these pursuits but be given a name related to what he has taken seriously.

Phaedrus: What names do you assign him?

Socrates: To call him a _wise_ person, Phaedrus, is too much, and only befitting a god, it seems to me. But a lover of wisdom or a name of this sort would be more appropriate and harmonious with his nature.

Phaedrus: And not at all contrary to his nature.[161]

Socrates: But, on the other hand, when a man possesses nothing more worthy than what he has arranged or written, endlessly turning his

e   pieces this way or that, putting bits together, then tearing them apart, won't you be completely within your rights to call him a poet[162] or prose-writer of speeches, or writer of laws?

Phaedrus: Yes, surely.

Socrates: Say these things, then, to your companion.

Phaedrus: What about you? What will you do? Certainly, it wouldn't be right at all for you to neglect your companion.

Socrates: Who's that?

---

158   Phaedrus has now been fully won over and persuaded.

159   Plato is probably quoting from Aristophanes' _Thesmophoriazusae_ which concludes with "we have played this out in a measured way."

160   The verb for arranging in this section is _syntithemi_, related to but not identical with the conventional noun used in rhetoric to discuss arrangement, _diathesis_ (cf. 228a).

161   _Apo tropou_, for this translation, I follow Thucydides (1.76); following Plato's _Republic_ (470b) and _Theaetetus_ (143c), de Vries translates: and nothing "beside the mark."

162   _poietes_. See Glossary under _Unskilled speaker_.

Phaedrus: The beautiful Isocrates. What will you report to him, Socrates? What shall we say he is?

Socrates: He's still young, Phaedrus, but I'm willing to say what I predict   279a
he will be called.

Phaedrus: What's this?

Socrates: His innate talent, I'd say, is at a higher level than anything we have seen in Lysias' speeches, and he also has a more noble character, so it wouldn't be that astonishing, in light of the speeches that he is now working on, if, as he matures, he dwarfed the work of his literary predecessors, but if the present pursuits should not satisfy him an even more divine passion might lead him to greater heights. For, my friend, a love of wisdom—of what sort, we can't judge yet—lies instinctively in the mind of that man.   b

I shall go to my darling Isocrates and deliver this report from the gods of this place, and you deliver your report to your darling Lysias.[163]

Phaedrus: Agreed. But let's be going, since now even the stifling heat is more gentle.

Socrates: Shouldn't we pray to the gods here before going?

Phaedrus: Yes, surely.

Socrates: Dear Pan and ye other gods who dwell here, grant that I become beautiful within and that my worldly belongings be in accord with my   c
inner self. May I consider the wise man rich and have only as much gold as a moderate man can carry and use.

Is there anything else we need, Phaedrus? For me, our prayer was said with due measure.

Phaedrus: Make it a prayer for me, too. Friends have things in common.

Socrates: Let's be going.

---

[163] Socrates says that Phaedrus is Lysias' lover at 236b5 (cf. 278e4) (as we learn from the palinode, lovers seek out like-souled people; 252c3-253c6), but in several instances in the dialogue, Socrates and Phaedrus (playfully) act as if Phaedrus has changed roles and is Socrates' beloved (243e4-8 and 261a 2-3; cf. 265c2-3).

INTERPRETATIVE ESSAY

A. The Head and Body of the *Phaedrus*

The *Phaedrus* has many beautiful parts, some of them among the most memorable in all of Plato's writings, but it remains a confusing dialogue, and it is far from simple to describe how, or if, the parts fit together into a coherent whole. The two main themes of the *Phaedrus* are rhetoric *and* love, and therein lies the difficulty. The problem of unity is all the more surprising since Socrates stresses in the dialogue that all compositions should be arranged like a unified organism:

> Every speech should be put together like a living creature with its own body so that it is not without a head or without a foot but has both a middle and extremities, written in such a way that its parts fit together and form a whole. (264c)

Though a dialogue is not a speech, like a speech it is a sophisticated rhetorical composition intended to persuade. Readers since antiquity have questioned what the head of the *Phaedrus* might be: rhetoric, love, the soul, divine beauty, philosophy (i.e., dialectic). Or if indeed it has a head. No doubt, the ambiguity is deliberate, Plato leaving it to the reader to ponder this question.

The dialogue also exhibits great shifts in tone. Near the middle of the *Phaedrus* Socrates offers a vision of the winged immortal soul. Like a charioteer drawn by an obedient white horse and an unruly dark one, she once traveled throughout the heavens in the company of the gods. But by an inevitable process of decay stemming from cowardice, wickedness, or forgetfulness, or possibly a combination of all three, the soul became heavy, lost its wings and fell to earth. There she landed in a human embryo and became earthbound. Only if her mortal bearer is smitten by the beauty of

73

another and overcome by an outpouring of desire will the soul begin to remember her former place among the gods. The stirrings of love cause the soul to sprout new wings, but like a fledgling she will be unable to fly until the mortal body dies and she is released from her bondage. Human beings untouched by love would regard such a person simply as mad, but Socrates understands that love-struck madness is divine, the person "having a god within" (cf. 249cd). Nowhere else in Plato is the image of divinity and transcendence so sustained, or the mystic ecstasy of reunification with divine Beauty through memory so vivid.

At the close of the speech, however, Phaedrus says almost nothing about this remarkable vision or even about love. He is thinking about the making of speeches, anxious that with this beautiful, impromptu speech Socrates has surpassed Lysias whom Phaedrus has long admired for his speech-writing. From this point forward until the end of the dialogue, Socrates leads his friend in a sober consideration of the properties of rhetoric. The shift from myth to reasoned dialectic is abrupt and a bit bewildering, as an outpouring of uninterrupted poetic and visionary language yields to a dialogue of proposition and critical scrutiny. Socrates proves to be a master at both forms of speech, as he himself seems to be aware, claiming after both his inspired vision (265c) and his discussion of rhetoric (278b) that he (and Phaedrus) have "played out" their discussion "with due measure." It remains to consider what Socrates means by "play," but for now we may wonder how the philosopher can master both forms of speech so skillfully and how these different parts of the dialogue fit into a coherent whole. First, the body.

I. The Body

Socrates' ecstatic speech is the last of three in the *Phaedrus*. It was not a speech he intended to make, but a series of events forced his hand. First, as we have seen, Phaedrus leads Socrates **outside the city gates (227b)**, on the pretext of practicing on Socrates a speech of Lysias which he has memorized. But Socrates sees the bulge under Phaedrus' cloak and forces him to read the speech itself.

Lysias' speech (230e-234c) is nominally about love, a subject dear to Socrates' heart, but the speech is also a rhetorical tour-de-force, a prime example of what the Athenians called an *epideictic* speech, a demonstration set piece designed to show off one's speaking prowess. In the spirit of that tradition and sophistic argumentation, Lysias tries to make the weaker argument appear stronger by employing plausible arguments for an implausible position, in this case by making a clever, if morally repugnant argument that the beloved should grant sexual favors to a non-lover. As we noted in the Introduction, he makes havoc of Greek pederastic convention where the older *erastes* and the younger *eromenos* enter into and enjoy the relationship for very different reasons. Without clearly stating his premise, Lysias implicitly accepts the Greek commonplace that a lover is an otherwise sane person driven mad by passion and feelings of jealousy. Free from all feelings of sexual desire, the beloved boy, Lysias implies, is drawn to an older man in the hope of forming a friendship. The boy is prone to pity the hapless lover but complies with his advances becuase of the material benefit and social rewards he expects to win from the relationship. If this is the case, Lysias asks, wouldn't it be more reasonable for the beloved to grant sexual favors to a non-lover who is cool-headed, rational, and free from possessive tendencies? What could be more sensible than to reward sexually the person who looks after one's material interests and social education? Compared to a lover, a non-lover makes a better manager of the beloved's interests, a better teacher and a better friend.

As this speech illustrates, Phaedrus believes that Lysias is "the most clever of our writers today." It is obvious to Phaedrus that the master rhetorician "spent so much time, in leisure, arranging" it (228a), Lysias' extensive labor in the composition being evident not only in the arrangement of the material but also in its argument. In praise, Phaedrus says: "Lysias has written about a beautiful boy and how he was pursued, but not by a lover, and it's just in this that Lysias was so refined" (227c).

Scholars debate whether the speech in this text is actually by Lysias or a Platonic parody of Lysias' style. I suspect parody. Phrases like "besides" and "and another thing" appear in many of Lysias' extant speeches but their frequency in this speech well exceeds anything found in that writer. But the more important point is that Plato incorporates a complete speech from a non-philosophical genre into the dialogue. As Andrea Nightingale describes this intrusion, "By making Lysias' speech the first in a series of three speeches, each of which supercedes its predecessor(s), Plato puts it in its place: the *logos* of Lysias appears simplistic, strained, and downright silly when compared with the other two speeches."[1]

After Phaedrus reads aloud "from the book" (243c), he turns to his companion: "Socrates, what do you think of the speech? Isn't it exceptional, both in its language and in other regards?" (234c). Far from it being the drug which will cure Socrates of his desire to hear speeches, **Socrates finds fault** with Lysias' speech and **is induced to make a speech of his own (234c-237a, 238c-d)**. At this point in the dialogue Socrates does not have a clear understanding of his objections, but he is beginning to formulate themes which will become increasingly important in the *Phaedrus*:

(1) Style, content, arrangement. Socrates introduces—perhaps for the first time in Greek literary history—a distinction between style and argument:

---

[1]   Nightingale, *Genres in Dialogue* (Cambridge, 1995) 154-55.

Must we praise the speaker for saying "what needed to be said, and not merely for the fact that each of its phrases was clear, compact, and well-turned?" (234e). In the second half of the dialogue, Socrates will criticize Lysias' speech for its arrangement: it mattered little what came first and what last (264e; cf. 235a). As Socrates articulates in his first speech and in the discourse on rhetoric, good speakers must define their subject, organize a speech with a head and organic coherence, and have the ability both to divide up an argument into its indivisible units and to collect them into a coherent whole.[2]

(2) Delivery: Socrates is certainly not intoxicated by Lysias' speech, but he is caught in a Bacchic frenzy and "lit up" by listening to Phaedrus read it (234d).[3] While it remains the case that Lysias' speech is a written text, Socrates' excitement from hearing his words read aloud anticipates his criticism of written texts at the end of the dialogue for being mere copies of extemporaneous speech which is alive and with soul (275d-276b).

(3) Archaic erotic poetry: Although he cannot say exactly how, Socrates' "chest feels full" like a reservoir with the poets Sappho and Anacreon, or perhaps even with some prose writers, whose words and knowledge he feels can help him make a better speech than Lysias'. Socrates will be the "vessel;" these "old and wise men and women [will be]...the foreign stream" flowing through him (235b-c). Such apparent acclaim for the poets is the first indication that Plato's quarrel with poetry in many of his other writings is in this dialogue muted, or even revoked. For the only time in Plato's writing, Socrates will begin his first speech by invoking the Muses for inspiration (237a). His opening words imitate the opening phrases of epic hymns and he will say in the context of that speech that he is speaking first in dithyrambic lyric and then in hexameter epic verse, as the hexameter rhythms of the last line of the speech testify. If Socrates is not altogether serious in these claims about his first speech, he also attributes his second speech to a lyric poet, Stesichorus, he recognizes his use of poetic language throughout, and he says he will hymn a song about the realm beyond the heavens which no poet (*poietes*) here on earth has ever sung before (247c). These acknowledged debts to poetry, especially in

---

2   For the need of definition, see 237b-d and 265d; for the need of a head and organizing principle, see 263d-264e; for division (*diairesis*) and collection (*sunagogos*), see 265e-266c and 277b. A number of critics argue that the real rival here is not Lysias but Isocrates (mentioned at the very end of the dialogue (279a-b), Plato's contemporary and rival. See Elizabeth Asmis, "*Psychagogia* in Plato's *Phaedrus*," *Illinois Classical Studies* XI (1986) 153-72. Cf. John Cooper, "Isocrates and Cicero on the Independence of Oratory from Philosophy," *Proceedings of the Boston Area Ancient Philosophy Colloquium* 1 (1985) 77-96.

3   Isocrates comments that speeches heard have much greater power than those read; cf. "To Philip" 24-29.

Socrates' second speech, have caused some to argue that in the *Phaedrus* Socrates recants his harsh rejection in the *Republic* of the Greek poetic tradition.[4]

But what about his particular acknowledgement of Sappho and Anacreon? The two are the originators and prime practitioners of Greek erotic poetry. Both sing primarily of same-sex love, Sappho usually of an older women for a younger one, and Anacreon of an *erastes* for an *eromenos*. In what way do the finest poets in the Greek erotic tradition provide the headwaters for Socrates' first speech which will be virulently anti-erotic? Some see the allusion as parody, the speech exaggerating the lover's madness, his pursuit and manipulation of the beloved in the poetic tradition. Others see the reference as looking beyond the narrow-minded question of gain and advantage in the first speech – a speech which Socrates already recognizes as misguided (242a) – and anticipating his later vindication of the poetic tradition in the second speech. Others go further and see in the reference to Sappho (but not to Anacreon), a model of female reciprocity between lover and beloved that is not found in traditional male erotic poetry (i.e., Anacreon). In these last two views, praise of poets before the first speech prepares the way for Socrates' seeming recognition in the second speech that the poetic tradition, if properly understood and transformed, can serve those who seek philosophic truth.[5]

(4) *poietes/idiotes*. Socrates may say that he speaks like a poet (*poietes*) but he also expressly calls himself an *idiotes*, saying that he is not a *poietes*. After his initial impulse to compete against Lysias, Socrates tries to back away from the challenge, protesting that an "unskilled speaker" like himself, an *idiotes*, speaking extemporaneously, would be a laughingstock go-

---

[4]   For the argument that in the *Phaedrus* Socrates recants his views in the *Republic* (387b, 607a), see Martha Nussbaum, *Fragility of Goodness* (Cambridge, 1986) 200-33; for a moderate view, see Christopher Janaway, *Images of Excellence: Plato's Criitique of the Arts* (Oxford, 1995) 162-69. Also see G. R. F. Ferrari, *Listening to the Cicadas: A Study of Plato's Phaedrus* (Cambridge, 1987) 113-19; cf. Marian Demos, *Lyric Quotation in Plato* (Lanham, Maryland, 1999) 65-86, who emphasizes that the theme of inspiration is stressed throughout the dialogue. Contrary to other Platonic dialogues, Socrates praises poetry inspired by divine madness (245a), but he also relegates poets to the sixth lowest category (out of nine) of mortal occupations (248e).

[5]   For the first view, see Christopher J. Rowe, Plato's *Phaedrus* (Warminster, 1986) 151; for the second, see R. Hackforth (tr.), Plato's *Phaedrus* (Cambridge, 1952) 36; Ronna Burger, Plato's *Phaedrus* (Birmingham, Alabama, 1980) 46; Nightingale (note 1) 158ff; for the third view, see Helene Foley, "'The Mother of the Argument': Eros and the Body in Sappho and Plasto's *Phaedrus*," in *Parchments of Gender* edited by M. Wyke (Oxford, 1988) 39-70. Also see Ferrari (note 4) 107-10 and Charles Griswold, *Self-Knowledge in Plato's Phaedrus* (New Haven, 1986) 53. Also see 255c and note 88 in the translation.

ing up against a "good speech-maker," an *agathos poietes*, like Lysias (236d). Socrates is using *poietes* here in its root sense of "maker" and begins what will be a continuous play in the dialogue on the meaning of this word. In deliberately ambiguous contexts, it is sometimes difficult to determine whether *poietes* refers to a maker/craftsman prose-writer or a (inspired) poet, as both speak "with measure." Like the philosopher in the *Symposium* who can master tragedy and comedy, Socrates will bridge categories: he is an extemporaneous speaker (*idiotes*) who speaks "in due measure" (*metrios*), with the language, vision, inspiration, and craft of a maker/poet (see the Glossary under *Unskilled speaker*).

(5) erotic competition: When Socrates, punning on Phaedrus' name ("Bright"), says that he is "lit-up" while listening to and observing him read, we get a hint of his affection for "the boy." He continues this punning in his second speech when he describes Zeus' love for Ganymede ("Bright-Counsel"). But contrary to his name, Phaedrus is rather dim-witted and undisciplined in aesthetic or philosophical judgment, which leaves open the question of why Socrates is drawn to him. In part, the answer lies in Phaedrus' special love for speeches, a love shared by Socrates. But it is probably fair to say that Socrates is attracted to all human beings, especially to males, not so much for their bodies as for the passion which is in them, and is eager to turn that passion toward a love of wisdom and the idea of the good. This is certainly the case with Phaedrus, whose soul, Socrates understands, is in crisis. Socrates is flirting with Phaedrus; some would go further and say (rightly, in my opinion) that he trying to seduce him. Socrates' motive for challenging Lysias by a speech of his own must be, at least in part, to win Phaedrus away from Lysias.[6]

Contrary to Lysias' written text, **Socrates' first speech (237a-241d)** is *impromptu*, delivered off the cuff without the "aid" of writing. Assuming the persona of a poet, he calls upon the liquid-tongued Muses to "come" and "take up his myth" (237a).[7] To keep the competition fair, Phaedrus insists that Socrates make the same argument as Lysias: i.e. that a non-lover keeps his head, while a lover can't and doesn't. Victory goes to superior arrangement (organization and development of argument) rather than to more clever argumentation (what Socrates calls "non-essential points," 236a). Aware that Lysias' speech was headless, Socrates begins

---

[6]   See David White, *Rhetoric and Reality in Plato's Phaedrus* (Albany, 1993) 13-7, and 170-73.

[7]   Socrates attributes this speech variously to the Nymphs (238d, 241e, 263d), to Dionysus (234d and 238d), to Phaedrus (who forced his hand) (244a), to Lysias (257d), and in ways only partially understood to the poets Sappho and Anacreon, or ancient prose writers (235b).

his speech with a statement about structure and argumentation, observing that for a speech to be successful it must open with a clear definition of its subject. Otherwise, a speaker will lose track of his topic: "Above all, my darling boy, there is only one way to begin for those who wish to deliberate successfully: they must know what they are deliberating about, or else completely miss the mark" (237c-d).[8]

Having firmly defined his subject, Socrates will concentrate on the love-sick lover as an irrational and untrustworthy person, jealous, unpleasant, and harmful to the beloved's body, property, and the education of his soul. There is nothing transcendent or uplifting about love in this speech. The lover is eager to keep his beloved weak and dependent; he is interested only in "immediate pleasures" (239a). He does everything in his power to "orphan" the beloved of things "most divine" (239e). The question is asked what "sting" keeps the beloved interested (240d) but no answer is given. In this attack against the lover (harmful, unpleasant, rapacious like wolves who adore lambs, 241d), Socrates is following Lysias' argument, but when it comes to praise the non-lover, he abruptly cuts short his speech.

Socrates' speech progresses by a series of necessities, both rhetorical and thematic: speeches must begin with a definition and build from it; lovers by necessity feel first one, then another emotion. Thus, love and rhetoric are joined in the recognition that both follow necessary rules and pathways.

Unlike Lysias who jumps from point to point, one sentence loosely joined to the next, Socrates builds his argument according to clearly constructed paragraphs, one building on the next. At this time in the evolution of Greek writing, there were no formal paragraph divisions, but the contrast in style between Lysias and Socrates' speeches is dramatic. One could just as easily design Lysias' speech as a single unbroken paragraph or as a series of short paragraphs, each a sentence or two long. By contrast, Socrates creates long units of thought which have a clear beginning and ending, prototypes of what later became paragraph units and a system of building up an argument with the logical succession of paragraph building blocks.

Socrates' speech is also superior to Lysias' philosophically in that it is composed extemporaneously for this particular occasion and designed for an audience of one, unlike a written text which can be picked up by any-

---

[8]   No one could disrupt the soundness of this advice if one's wish is to make a strong formal argument, but Socrates' approach may be questioned if one's intent is to seduce a wavering beloved.

one. As we will learn in the discussion on rhetoric, true philosophy and the reaching of souls through language only truly works one on one.

From the beginning to the end of this speech, Socrates speaks with his head covered by his cloak,[9] aware from the start, we must presume, that his words are shameful. This gesture anticipates his later **repudiation of the speech (242c-243e)**. As he brings it to a halt, he longs to leave the grove, but his private spirit forbids Socrates from crossing the river before he has purified himself for his error. It is not a fault of style or argument, but of substance, for having slandered a god in order to win honor among men. To appease the gods, he must make a retracting speech, or **"palinode," (243e-257b)** in praise of Eros, the god of Love.

According to Socrates' criteria, speeches may be evaluated along three lines: style, manner and appropriateness of argumentation (partly stylistic, partly formal), and content (i.e., the truth of the assertions made). Lysias' written text exemplified the first quality; Socrates' first speech the second quality; his palinode will emphasize the third.

Even more than his first speech, the palinode is filled with poetic vision and poetic language. Socrates' image of the winged soul in the company of the gods beyond heaven reveals what no earthly poet has described before (247c). He attributes the entire speech to the archaic poet, Stesichorus (Standing-Chorus), son of Good-Speech (Euphemos), from the Land of Desire (Himera), a real figure made blind like Homer for slandering Helen. Unlike Homer, Stesichorus offered a *palinode* and regained his sight. Like Socrates' first speech, the palinode offers a definition but only after a lengthy and intricately-crafted introduction. As a prelude to his main theme, Socrates feels compelled: (1) to describe three different kinds of divine madness which benefit humankind (244a-245c); (2) to argue, in the manner of a pre-Socratic philosopher, for the immortality of the soul (245c-246a); (3) to describe the form of the soul by comparing her to a charioteer who commands an obedient white horse and a frisky black one (246a-249d); (4) to praise erotic madness as the fourth and highest form of divine madness (249d-e). Only then does the definition follow: "he is called a lover when as a lover of beautiful things he shares in this madness" (249e). In formal structure, the palinode follows the principle of composition that Socrates outlined in his first speech, even as it exceeds in sophistication the structure of that speech. But in his attention to content, Socrates has next to nothing to say about arrangement or argumentation. Surely this is not accidental. The point seems to be that when Socrates speaks for himself

---

[9]   237a; cf. 242c and 243b.

(i.e., not competitively against Lysias) he achieves truth and form, even while overt attention to rhetoric drops from view.[10] Fittingly, he delivers the palinode with his head uncovered.

The tone and language in the palinode, as noted above, exceed anything found in the rest of Plato, and certainly differ from the earlier part of the dialogue. The myth proper begins with a vision of the soul in her heavenly realm before she loses her wings, falls to earth, and takes on a body (246a-250c). The myth or fable proceeds with one of Plato's most famous images, likening the form of the unencumbered soul to a pair of horses (one white, the other black) driven by a charioteer. In the course of his narration Socrates "hymns" the praises, as no poet here on earth has ever done or ever will do, of the "place beyond heaven," the realm of Being and the Forms, which is colorless, shapeless, untouchable, invisible but to the mind, "the soul's pilot." It is the place of all true knowledge and the only place where the soul is nourished as she contemplates the truth in joyous passion (247c-d). The only way for the earth-bound soul to revisit heaven is through *recollection* (*anamnesis*).[11]

Recollection, in this myth, is a by-product of love, divinely-given, when a lover is caught by the physical beauty of a beloved. The beauty of the beloved enters through the eyes and stirs the soul, causing the stalks of the fallen wings to swell and to feel the urge to rise, and *reminding* (*hypomnesis*) the best of souls of their time in heaven. Most lovers cannot see beyond the earthly pleasure and the "unnatural" desire "to mount and to spawn children according to the law of a four-footed animal" (250e), but for a special few the boy's beauty will *remind* the soul of the true and invisible heavenly beauty and stir the wing stalks throbbing (251a-252c). *Anamnesis* works through *hypomnesis*: "only a man who correctly handles such *reminders* and is ever initiated into the perfect mysteries is truly perfect" (249c).[12] By means of these reminders, he is able to "pick up the habits and practices [of a god] to the extent that humans can share in the divine" (253a).

---

[10]   See the excellent discussion of these points in Paul Friedländer, *Plato*, vol. I, *An Introduction*, Chapter 3, "The Written Word," tr. Hans Meyerhoff, Bollingen Series LIX (New York, 1958) 108-25.

[11]   *Anamnesis*, whereby human beings can "recollect" (usually through reasoned dialectic) the world of Ideas and true Being, is a central tenet in many of Plato's writings.

[12]   The noun *anamnesis* only appears once in the *Phaedrus* (249c2), but the verb three times (249d6 and 250a1, as well as 275a4-5). The noun *hypomnesis* only appears at 249c7, the verb appears again at 275a5.

Contrary to other forms of *anamnesis* in Plato's writings, in this myth recollection depends on divine madness. The lover/philosopher must be "seized" and "captured" by love (252c), as Zeus seized the mortal Ganymede and carried him to heaven (cf. 255c). Such souls are "driven out of their senses" (*ekplettontai*) and "lose self-possession" (*ouket en hauton gignontai*), no longer masters of themselves (250a), traits which go far beyond the characteristics of *amamnesis* in other Platonic writings. The common verb for this possession in the *Phaedrus* is *enthousiazein*, literally "to have the god within" (or "to be enthused").

Anyone who shies away from the risk of this erotic mania runs the risk of prolonged impoverishment. In language almost unattested in the rest of Plato, Socrates assaults mortals smug in their petty ratiocinations. A prime example of such a figure is the non-lover praised in Lysias' speech and implicitly in Socrates' first speech (237e). Socrates acknowledges that true moderation (one which does not turn its back on erotic madness) belongs on a pedestal with divine Beauty (cf. 254b, 247d). Mortal moderation, on the other hand, which shuns divine madness even while seeking to gain the favor of the beloved, is severely scorned, as quoted above: intimacy, diluted by mortal moderation, pays meager mortal dividends and begets in his companion's soul a slavish economizing which most people praise as a virtue but which will in fact cause the soul to roam for 9,000 years, around the earth and beneath it, mindlessly (cf. 256e-257a).

The palinode ends with a **prayer to Eros (257a-b)**. Socrates begins the prayer by referring to his speech as a gift to Love: "This, my dear Eros, is the finest and most beautiful palinode within my powers" (257a). Some place great weight on "within my powers," as if Socrates were stressing the fact that in this speech, unlike his first speech when he said he was possessed by the Nymphs of the grove and by Dionysos (241e), he is in full possession of his faculties, relying solely upon his own abilities. Others, rightly in my opinion, feel the effect of the grove is still upon Socrates and question whether Socrates could have envisioned the place of Being beyond heaven if he had not been led out of the city to this charmed spot. Trees, after all, do have something to teach the city philosopher. Even after the palinode, however, Socrates continues to "blame" these nymphs and the cicadas singing in the plane tree overhead for his "gift" of eloquence (262d; cf. 263d).[13]

---

[13]   Socrates clearly emphasizes that mortals must lose self-possession to gain the rewards of divine possession, and that poetry and song without divine possession, poetry composed by skill or art alone, falls short of its goal (cf. 245a), but he never says explicitly that he is inspired as he delivers the palinode.

The prayer concludes with Socrates' concern for his companion, a man, as we saw above, who Socrates says is "going in two directions."

Phaedrus joins in the prayer, although with little commitment, it appears ("I join with you in that prayer, Socrates, if this will really be better for us," 257b). Phaedrus says that he is astonished by Socrates' palinode for its beauty but it is shocking that he fails to ask Socrates one question after that extraordinary speech, although by the end of the dialogue Phaedrus seems to be completely won over by Socrates (at least for the moment).[14] With this, the dialogue turns abruptly to a discussion about **written texts** and **rhetorical theory (258d-279b)**, beginning with the question: what makes for good or bad compositions (258d; 259e).

As with his speeches, Socrates begins the conversation with a definition:

> Isn't the art of rhetoric, taken as a whole, a certain guiding of souls through words, not only in the law courts and other places of public assembly but also in private? Doesn't the same art deal with major and minor matters and is it any more honorable, if correctly employed, when used in serious matters than when used in trivial ones? (261a-b).

This definition of rhetoric is unlike any other in Plato or in the rest of Greek literature, and it catches Phaedrus completely by surprise: "No, by god, [rhetoric is] not at all the way you described it." Two aspects of the definition must have shocked Phaedrus. The first is to claim that the art is "a certain guiding of souls" (*psychagogia tis*), since the convention of the day looked upon soul-guiding in negative terms. Such business was associated with conjuring up souls from the dead, or in the context of speech with persuasion through witchcraft and phantasms. Phaedrus is no less shocked to hear Socrates, contrary to all the handbooks of the day, take rhetoric out of the lawcourts and public assemblies and associate it with one-on-one discourse. [15] Both moves are crucial to the dialogue.

The philosopher depends on rhetoric to reach another soul and turn her away from the things of this world toward a love of wisdom, truth, and beauty. By the time Socrates repeats his definition of rhetoric, *psychagogia* applied to rhetoric no longer seems so strange to Phaedrus. Witness Socrates' refined definition:

> Since the capacity of speech is to *guide the soul*, someone intending to become a rhetorician must know what forms the soul possesses. The number of forms is so and so; their quality such and such; hence people are of this sort and others of that sort. When these divisions are made, he needs again to know that the forms of speeches are so and so and

---

[14]   Cf. 278b5-6 and 279c6-7.
[15]   For both points, see note 106 in the translation.

the quality of each such and such. Therefore, people of this sort can be easily persuaded by such and such for this or that reason to do one thing or another...(271c-d)

And Phaedrus' replies: "It is not possible to describe it otherwise, Socrates, I suppose" (272b). It may be possible to apply the later definition of rhetorical training to speeches before large crowds, although it is difficult to see how. Ideally it pertains to intimate exchanges between two people. A true rhetorician is more likely to practice his art sitting under a plane tree by a river than in the Pnyx before the assembled Athenian citizenry. The real art, or *tekhne*, of rhetoric pertains more to philosophy than to demagoguery and more to one-on-one discourse than to epideictic speech.[16]

Also, as is becoming increasingly clear, reasoned rhetoric and divinely sent love have one crucial element in common: the capacity, if handled correctly, to turn souls toward a love of wisdom and the beautiful.[17]

A further surprise in Socrates' account of this art comes at the climax of his several descriptions of rhetoric.[18] The purpose of the art is not to persuade or charm humankind, but to gratify the gods:[19] "A moderate man

---

[16]   For example, "Until [a person) sees thoroughly into the nature of the soul according to these same principles, discovering the form that most fits each nature, and accordingly makes and arranges his speech, supplying intricate or multi-colored speeches, covering all the harmonic modes for an intricate or multi-colored soul and supplying simple speech for a simple soul, [not until then] will he be able to manage the class of speeches artfully..." (277c).

[17]   Stylistically, the discourse about rhetoric and art has fallen off considerably from the palinode, but the philosophic argument about speech has advanced beyond the myth of the palinode. Two features exhibited "by chance" in the palinode prove essential to the discussion of this art: division (*diairesis*) and collection (*synagoge*) of thought (see note 2).

[18]   Four passages identify what one must know to become skilled in the art of rhetoric: 270c9-d7 (what one must know about all living things), 271a4-b5 (regarding rhetoric); 271c10-272b4 (the beginning of which is quoted above); 273d2-274a5 (the end of which is quoted in this paragraph). A recapitulation or summary (an *epanodos*?; cf. 267e4) can be found at 277b5-c6. See Griswold (note 5) 186-97.

[19]   In *Against the Sophists* 13.16-17, Isocrates argues that a good rhetorician must "choose the forms (*eidea*) that are necessary for each subject...mix...and arrange (*tazei*) them properly, not miss the right opportunities (*kairon*)...and speak rhythmically and musically (*eurythmos kai mousikos*)." Socrates agrees with each of these criteria and some of the terminology but adds the necessity of knowing the soul type of his listener and the (divine) purpose of speech. On all but this last point, see Asmis (note 2) 167-69. The same arguments and terminology found in Isocrates' speech are also used by the other side in the heated fourth-century debate over the relative merits of written texts and extemporaneous speech, as illustrated in Alkidamas' "On those who write written speeches" (especially sections 27-34). See Appendix D.

does not put himself through this labor in order to speak and to act in the company of human beings, but to put himself in a position to say what is gratifying to the gods and at all times to act in a gratifying manner to the best of his ability…[For] men wiser than us say that a man of intelligence must not concern himself with gratifying fellow slaves, except in a secondary way, but rather with gratifying masters who are good and from good stock" (273e-274a).

But, it becomes increasingly obvious that no human being can become a true rhetorician. The demands of the art exceed human capacity. Not even the most astute philosopher can know the nature of all souls and the variety of speeches appropriate to each soul. In his conclusion of the art, Socrates hints at the immensity of the task: "So, if the circuit is long, don't be astonished." Phaedrus catches what he means: "That's said very beautifully, it seems to me, Socrates, if only anyone could do it" (274a). As the *Republic* acknowledges that it is impossible to build the just city here on earth, so in this dialogue Socrates recognizes that even if humans cannot master the art of rhetoric the effort is ennobling: "And yet even in reaching for the beautiful there is beauty, and also in suffering whatever it is that one suffers en route" (274a-b) … "To call [a highly skilled and knowledgeable speaker] *wise*, Phaedrus, is too much and only befitting a god…But a lover of wisdom or a name of this sort would be more appropriate and harmonious with his nature" (278d).

The conversation on rhetoric does not draw to a close with a discussion of style, arrangement, or content but with myth and a **detour to Egypt (274c-275d)** where Socrates tells his companion about the invention of writing, an ancient tale which he once heard someone tell. The invention of letters is credited to **Theuth** (probably a variation of the Egyptian god Thoth, in the Greek pantheon analogous to Hermes, a *psychopomp* or leader of souls in his own right). The inventor presents the alphabet to the god **Thamus** (also called Ammon and analogous to Zeus), who is king of the Upper Kingdom (literally, the Upper Place). Proud of his invention, Theuth wishes his letters to be distributed to all the people, believing that he has discovered the *pharmakon*, a drug or remedy, for memory (*mnesis*) and wisdom. But the king, acting as judge, pronounces sentence, however, that the invention will cause forgetfulness; the *pharmakon* is thus more a poison than a remedy, and should be kept from the people. In his pronouncement, the king distinguishes recollection of essential things (*anamnesis*) from reminding (*hypomnesis*) and places writing in the second category. But unlike the palinode where recollection works through reminding, the king says that writing endangers recollection, causing true memory to wither. Socrates broadly concurs with Thamus, criticizing writing for being a frozen, unresponsive copy of living language. In true face-to-face rhetoric, a speaker selects his partner and shapes his discourse "with knowledge" (276a and e) according to the nature of his companion's soul. Writing is tolerable so long as one is aware that it is a game, play-acting and not serious, a mere reminder of what one already knows through philosophic dialectic. (I shall return to this topic and consider its relevance to Plato's own writing in section E of the Essay.)

The *Phaedrus* ends much as the palinode did, with a **prayer**, here **to Pan (279b-c)** and the other gods of this grove. Both are prayers that the soul be guided in the right direction; in this case that Socrates be beautiful within, that his outer self be in harmony with his inner being, and that he desire only as much gold as a moderate man can carry and use. Phaedrus asks that the prayer be made for him as well, as friends share things in common.

An overview: As Seth Benardete writes: "The initial puzzle for anyone who reads the *Phaedrus* is the ultimate puzzle."[20] This puzzle is the question of unity, or what Benardete calls the nonevident unity. Socrates, it would appear (cf. 262c10 and 265c8-d1), divides the dialogue into two (relatively equal) parts, the first consisting of speeches (on love), the second of a discussion about the making of speeches. As Anne Lebeck describes the **diptych**: "These two forces, Eros and Logos, are complements of one another: both lead the soul to ultimate harm or good."[21]

But to divide the *Phaedrus* between Eros and Logos lumps the three speeches into one, as if the palinode were of a piece with the other two, when in fact it jumps out at the reader for its fervor and its myth in the midst of a surrounding sobriety. Indeed, it is different from almost all other Platonic writing.[22] From this perspective it might be more reasonable to think of the *Phaedrus* as a **triptych**, the palinode framed on either side by rhetorical considerations.

---

[20]   Benardete, *The Rhetoric of Morality and Philosophy: Plato's Gorgias and Phaedrus* (Chicago, 1991) 103. In answer to the question whether a perfect writing is like an animal, he writes: "The *Phaedrus*, however, might not have a human shape and still be rational. It might look like a monster only because we are too much into ourselves and have not yet stepped out of our skins" (p. 105).

[21]   Lebeck, "The Central Myth of Plato's *Phaedrus*," *Greek, Roman, and Byzantine Studies* 13 (1972) 268.

[22]   The first two speeches are as much about rhetoric as they are about love. In the discussion of true rhetoric, Socrates and Phaedrus occasionally draw from the previous speeches in the *Phaedrus* to illustrate a point, but when this happens, almost invariably reference is made to Lysias' speech or to Socrates' first speech. The remarkable qualities of Socrates' second speech go for the most part without comment in the second half of the dialogue, except perhaps at 258e-259e. See difficulties at 262cd.

II. The Head

In terms of character, time, and place (Aristotle's categories for unity), the *Phaedrus* is clearly of one piece and forms a whole. The problem arises in its "strikingly juxtaposed verbal paths," to adopt Ferrari's happy phrase:[23] myth and dialectic, poetry and dialogue, narrowly pragmatic and visionary views.

Some would say that Plato failed to join these distinct paths—eros and logos, myth and dialectic—around a unifying theme. The *Phaedrus* should be enjoyed for its parts, but not as a whole. Others argue that eros is subordinated to rhetoric. Still others argue that the ancient Greeks were more tolerant of diverse themes loosely joined than are moderns.[24] Even if this is the case, we still need to recall Socrates' injunction in the dialogue that a speech have a (single) head.

A fourth possibility is that the *Phaedrus* has a hybrid design to suit Phaedrus' nature. At the beginning of the dialogue, Socrates questions whether his own soul is beast-like: I "inquire...about myself [to see] whether I happen to be some sort of beast even more various in form and more overweening than the hot-blooded Typhon, or something tamer and simpler" (230a). Undoubtedly, all human beings have complex, even savage souls. In the *Republic*, for example, Socrates says: "to be sure some terrible, savage, and lawless form of desires is in every man, even in some of us who seem to be ever so measured, [all subject to appetites] which reveal themselves most readily in dreams" (9.572b) (underlining mine).[25] But in this dialogue, Socrates does not appear to be Typhon-like; Phaedrus, by

---

[23]   Ferrari (note 4) 34.

[24]   For the supremacy of rhetoric, see C. J. Rowe, "The Unity of the *Phaedrus*: A Reply to Heath," *Oxford Studies in Ancient Philosophy* 7 (1987) 175-88; for Greek tolerance of diversity, Malcolm Heath, *Unity in Greek Poetics* (Oxford, 1990), and "The Unity of Plato's *Phaedrus*," *Oxford Studies in Ancient Philosophy* 7 (1989) 151-73 and 189-91, although he says very little about the "single head" passage in the *Phaedrus*.

[25]   Nietzsche speaks well about this side of Socrates in "The Problem of Socrates" in *Twilight of the Idols*. While the last scene in the *Symposium* reveals a calm Socrates who is inoculated against all forms of intoxication, statements like this one in the *Republic* suggest a monstrous core. But like the charioteer of the soul whom Socrates describes in the palinode, he has been able to turn his soul in the right direction and thus has made his soul simpler and less bestial than that of the hybrid and monstrous Typhon.

contrast, is "going in two directions."[26] Socrates adapts his conversation, so this line of argument would have it, to suit the complex nature of Phaedrus' soul.

But, as ancient and modern readers have also observed, the recurrence of theme, image and words throughout the dialogue offers a fifth and ultimately more attractive approach. The discussions of love and rhetoric can belong to the same dialogue because both require the philosopher at the helm. As a lover, the philosopher guides the soul of the beloved; as a rhetorician, he guides the soul of his partner in conversation. One speaks through mythic hymns and poetic language, the other through dialectical speech. As Ferrari says: [Plato] "allows neither path to reach a satisfactory goal; rather, one leads only to the other. If we want Plato's view on the philosophy displayed but not anaysed in the dialogue's second part we must turn to the first; but there his view is presented only mythically...It is just the kinship in limitation of these otherwise very different paths of discourse, myth and argument—at least when the philosopher confronts his own art—that is of such philosophic interest" (p. 34). Charles Griswold praises the dialogue for much the same reason: in Socrates, reason and madness converge.[27]

The head of the dialogue, then, is not so much a single passage as a motivating idea, that of turning the soul, through love or rhetoric, and guiding her toward a love of wisdom and the idea of the good. If the *Phaedrus* does indeed have a single head, as I think it does, it should be considered this, soul-turning.[28]

---

26   In the *Republic*, "going in two directions" describes creatures or things which are multiple, both beautiful and ugly, big and small. Such is the nature of Phaedrus' soul: complex rather than simple, and far from tamed.

27   Griswold (note 5) 2 and 151-65. On the question of the *Phaedrus'* head, see Nightingale (note 1).

28   For a summary discussion of these positions, see R. B. Rutherford *The Art of Plato* (Cambridge, Mass., 1995) 260-67. Rutherford concludes his thoughts on unity as follows (a point of view, it should become clear, with which I am not in full agreement): "That Plato praises unity in a work which seems to most readers baffling, diverse and varied in matter and tone is neither coincidence nor incompetence, but deliberate; it points to the imperfections of the written word, to the unfinished nature of this, and every, treatment of philosophic themes. It also reflects the complex and non-simple natures of the participants. Whatever is the case with Socrates, the *Phaedrus* is complex in part because Phaedrus himself is complex and divided; and if the discussion in the second half seems rambling and peculiar, or if the second half as a whole seems to fail to live up to the promise of the Palinode, that may be related to the fact that Socrates eventually failed with Phaedrus" (266-67). For another view of unity, see Jesper Svenbro, *Phrasikleia: An Anthropology of Reading in Ancient Greece.* tr. Janet Lloyd (Ithaca, 1993) 199-210.

For lover and rhetorician, the nature of the soul's journey obviously differs. Physical beauty in the sensible world awakens through divine madness memories of divine Beauty in the invisible realm seen only with the mind's eye as well as a discovery of the god within himself (252e-253a). The lover will then lead the beloved to the god, causing that soul to rediscover herself (253bc). The rhetorician, no less, first "discovers" through reasoned dialectic "the discourses within himself" (what Socrates calls "his legitimate sons") (278a), before he leads the soul of a friend, whether in speech or conversation, toward a love of wisdom and gratification of the gods. The two journeys are exemplified in the figure of Phaedrus who is "astonished by" Socrates' palinode (257c)[29] and won over by his treatise on true rhetoric (278b).

B. Language and Imagery

There is imagistic unity as well. The *Phaedrus* is no less a work of art than a philosophical text, and a full reading of the dialogue requires literary skills of tracing verbal repetition and imagistic patterning. As with poetry, word and image gain in meaning as they re-echo in the dialogue. Such compression often exposes ambiguity and the contradictory nature of everyday speech. An Aeschylean scholar writing on Socrates' palinode describes the experience of reading the *Phaedrus* this way: "Like the lover gazing upon the beloved, [the reader] is excited by the iridescence of the language, stimulated by points of light which appear and disappear. In this way is initiated an experience which could be crowned with insight. Thus the dialogue itself is *Phaedrus*, bright with beauty, inducing insight by that beauty."[30]

In the *Phaedrus* conventional phrasing used before the palinode turns bold in the palinode itself. For example, the playful image of speeches as banquets (227b, 230d, 236e) before Socrates' second speech takes on a thematic urgency in the palinode when the feathers of the soul, and the soul herself, are described as nourished by sight of the divine when "banqueting upon...the things that really are"(247e; ccf. 246e, 248b, etc.). Similarly, to describe the "resting place" along the Ilissos where Phaedrus and Socrates sit down as a *katagoge* (literally, a "bringing down") is suggestive. It is not a common word in classical Athens, though twice used in this dialogue (230b and 259a, in its adjectival form) but nowhere else in Plato's extant writings. In light of the central myth of the *Phaedrus* about the immortal soul falling down (*kata*) from heaven to earth and through

---

[29] In spite of Socrates' prediction at 238d that Phaedrus would be astonished by his first speech, it is not until he hears Socrates' palinode that he expresses astonishment.

[30] Lebeck (note 21) 290.

love and language having the capacity to make an upward ascent (*agein ano*) ("lifting weighty things heavenward, roaming through the stars where the race of the gods dwell," 246d), the literal meaning of *katagoge* should not be ignored. The commonplace image of the lover as someone "being moved" (*tou kekinemenou*, 245b) fits into the same theme as does the theme of movement in the second half of the dialogue..[31] Delightfully, the *Phaedrus* ends with a plea for movement" "Let's be going" (*iomen*, 279c8).

In this densely packed language, one image is fused with another; in this case, the idea of movement is intermixed with language of initiation. A word like *ateles* which early in the palinode means "imperfect" or "incomplete" (245a) in the context of souls comes to mean "uninitiated" into the spectacle of Being (248b), but in the context of the philosopher, without the negating "alpha" it refers to one who is perfect and initiated into the mysteries (cf. 250bc). The language is so layered in some passages that it defies translation: "only a man who correctly handles such reminders and is ever initiated into these perfect mysteries, is truly perfect." The verbosity of my translation attempts to render the untranslatable *teleous aei teletas teloumenos, teleos ontos monos gignetai* (249c).[32]

Words similarly reverberate throughout the dialogue around questions of writing, extempore speaking, memory, and "measured" language. At this time in Athens, it would have been very rare to read a speech as Phaedrus does to Socrates under the plane tree. But there was a great aesthetic clash between "live" extemporaneous speech and the carefully crafted written

---

31   The second half of the dialogue reworks the imagery of movement in a number of ways, including Socrates' belief that rhetoric is a "method or approach" (*methodos*), but not along the path to be found in Lysias and Thrasymachos: an approach that lacks full knowledge of the proper use of rhetorical elements and of the addressee's soul is like "like a blind man's journey" (269d and 270d, respectively). Such knowledge is hard to come by: "so, if the circuit (*periodos*) is long, don't be astonished. For great things, one must take the long way around (*periiteon*)" (274a). (*Periodos* echoes the word describing the circuit which the soul takes in company with the gods in the realm beyond heaven, 247d, 248c, 249a.) Cf. Lebeck (note 21) 284-85.

32   The multiple meanings of *telos* (used twice) (to refer to an "initiate" into a mystery or revelation of sacred things as well as to someone who is "perfect or complete," in the sense of realizing to the full one's moral and spiritual capabilities), of the related noun *teletas* and of the participle *teloumenos* make this passage virtually impossible to translate. See Lebeck (note 21) 269-80. The second half of the dialogue reworks this imagery as well: "if your natural abilities fall short [of mastering all necessary rhetorical skills and knowledge], you'll be less than perfect (*ateles*)" (269d); cf. plants which, if properly sowed, reach their full and mature form (276b). Also see the Glossary under *Initiation*.

text. There was in Athens a deep-seated bias for extempore speech. If less artful, it spoke to the moment. Polished speech garnered suspicion of mendacity and costly coaching. On the other hand, Athenians greatly admired the stylistic flourish that came with training and patient workmanship. The commonplace term for the polished writer was *poietes logon*, "a crafter of words."[33]

Socrates cuts through this aesthetic divide. Early in the dialogue, he calls himself an *idiotes*, a word which originally referred to an unexceptional citizen not engaged in the public arena, but here describes someone who is unskilled and untrained, in short, an amateur. Lysias, by contrast, is a *poietes* (234e and 236d), which here does not mean poet but skilled craftsman, a professional. Explicit in this contrast is the divide between extempore speech and writing: "I'll be a laughing stock," Socrates complains, "unskilled and improvising on the spot going up against a fine maker of speeches" (236d; Phaedrus uses similar language to contrast his impromptu amateurism to Lysias' crafted professionalism at 228a).[34] By the end of the dialogue, however, Socrates will have demonstrated that he is a master of both extempore and "measured" speech, revealing to the reader how the philosopher absorbs and transcends apparent contradictions, in much the same way as in the *Symposium* he argues that the philosopher must absorb and transcend the apparent differences between tragedy and comedy. He turns this trick in the *Phaedrus* by an endlessly playful twist and turn in meaning for words like *poietes* and *metrios*.

First, as much as Socrates calls himself an *idiotes*, he makes it clear throughout the dialogue that he is also a *poietes*. In the palinode, he says that he will describe the place beyond heaven which no other *poietes* here on earth has praised in song (247c). Here, he uses the word in its conventional sense to mean poet. He also indicates that poets spur him on to challenge Lysias (235c-d). He begins his first speech as if he were a poet when he invokes the Muses (237a), something Socrates does nowhere else in Plato. During that speech he says he is speaking in dithyrambic meters (238c-d), then in epic hexameter (241e), as is confirmed by the hexameter

---

[33]   Cf. Johan Schloemann, "Entertainment and Democratic Distrust: The Audience's Attitudes towards Oral and Written Oratory in Classical Athens," in *Epea and Grammata* edited by Ian Worthington and John Miles Foley. *Mnemosyne Suppl.* 230 (Leiden, 2002) 133-46.   Also see Appendix D.

[34]   Plato's contemporary and rival Isocrates uses *poietes* and *idiotes* in much the same way to distinguish a professional prose *writer* (who teaches political writing: *politikous logous*) from an unskilled, *improvising* verbal bumbler; cf. Isocrates, "Against the Sophists" 13.9. This tract, written about 390 BCE when Isocrates was 46, came at the outset of his career as a teacher of rhetoric. For Isocrates, there is a political undertone in the word *poietes* which is absent from the *Phaedrus* as it has little interest in public rhetoric.

ending to his speech (241d). He attributes his second speech to the poet Stesichorus (243e-244a) and admits at the end of that speech that his language throughout has been "poetical" (*poietika*) (257a5). He also breaks into verse three times.[35]

In the second half of the dialogue, his use of *poietes* is more bold, as is his play with the word for measure and verse, *metron*. The argument requires close attention to wording. The first tease comes when Socrates describes a *poietes* leaving the *theatron*. The passage has caused translators fits. In one recent translation, *poietes* is treated metaphorically: "he leaves the *stage* a poet." But as other translators have realized, *poietes* cannot mean poet here, but speech writer, a fact which makes the translation of *theatron* difficult: one translator offers "the *author* quits the *scene*"; another "the composer leaves the assembly."[36]

Just a few lines later, Socrates compounds the verbal playfulness. Considering how one can tell whether someone writes well or poorly, Socrates asks:

> How, then, do you write well or poorly? Phaedrus, should we cross-examine Lysias about these things, and anyone else who has ever written, or intends to write anything, whether it be a political or private written work (*syngramma*), whether he writes *en metro hos poietes e aneu metrou hos idiotes*? (258d)

The translation appears simple enough, until the last word: "in verse as a poet or without verse as an *idiotes*." The Greek-English dictionary does not help, claiming as it does that *idiotes* here means "prose writer," although it offers no parallels and this meaning is diametrically opposed, as we have seen, to its meaning of "extemporaneous speaker" earlier in the dialogue. Nor is it particularly obvious why Socrates should introduce the contrast between a poet and prose writer at this point in the discussion. His focus is on written, prose composition (*syngramma*) and statesmen—Lykourgos, Solon, Darius, only one of whom is a poet (Solon).

---

[35]   Cf. 243a, 252b, 264d.

[36]   For *ek tou theatrou ho poietes* (258b3). In this passage Socrates is clearly describing a political speaker who addresses a crowd or the Council, a figure he has just called a "prose writer"(*syngrapheus*) who sometimes composes (*poiesamenos*) an extraordinarily long written text (*syngramma*) (258a). The translations above are those of Nehamas and Woodruff, Hackforth, and Reale ("il compositore se ne va dall'assemblea"), respectively. My offering: "the maker of speeches leaves the theater rejoicing."

Translators understandably struggle with the passage. One offers: "Is it incumbent on us, Phaedrus, to examine Lysias on this point, and all such as *have written or mean to write anything at all,* whether in the field of *public or private,* whether *in the verse of the poet or the plain speech of prose.*" Another: "Do we need to ask this question of Lysias or anyone else *who ever did or will write anything—whether a public or private document, poetic verse or plain prose.*"[37] At the center of this word play is the term *metron.* The *poietes* has it; the *idiotes* by definition does not. For reasons I shall now explain, I translate: "whether he writes with measure like a speech-maker or without measure like an unskilled speaker."

The ultimate play, I suspect, is on the word *metrios.* Socrates, the *idiotes,* repeatedly describes himself as speaking *metrios,* an adverb which can mean "moderately," "within due limits," or "enough," "pretty well." At first glance, the word appears casual and conventional when Phaedrus comments that Socrates has spoken *metrios* (236a). Later, as the word is repeated, it accumulates weight. After the palinode Socrates says that his "mythic hymn" was said *metrios te kai euphemos,* "with due measure and reverence" (265c). Hymns, of course, are traditionally in poetic form. The term is particularly noteworthy at the end of the dialogue when in a flurry it describes Socrates' speech:

> At 277b, I translate: "I'd say that we have shown *in due measure (metrios)* what is made with art and what is not." Others translate: "Now, I think, we have *pretty well* cleared up the question of art," or "Now, I think that we have answered that question *clearly enough.*"

> At 278b, I translate: "Well, then, we have played out our discussion of speeches *in a measured way.*" Others translate: "Then we may regard our literary pastime as *having reached a satisfactory conclusion,*" or "Well, then, our playful amusement regarding discourse is *complete.*"

> At 279c (in almost the last words of the dialogue), I translate: "For me, our prayer was said *with due measure*" (279c). Others translate: "The prayer *contents* me," or "I believe my prayer is *enough* for me."

The repetition of *metrios* is striking and needs emphasis. As a speaker, Socrates is an *idiotes,* as he must be, for philosophy depends upon one-on-one "living" speech. But Socrates is a *poietes* in both senses: he speaks with a poet's art and inspired vision and he is a craftsman who composes in measured speech.

---

[37] The first is by Hackforth (the Greek has *hos* = "as", not "of"), the second by Nehamas and Woodruff.

Plato's rival, Isocrates, prided himself for composing like a poet "with music and rhythms" (*meta mousikes kai rhythmon*) and "with rather poetic and elaborate phrasing" (*poietikotera kai poikilotera*).[38] All rhetoricians, he believed, should compose "rhythmically and musically" (*eurythmos kai mousikos*).[39] Like the Socrates of the *Phaedrus*, he also argued that rhetoricians should arrange elements of a speech into a fitting whole and that rhetoricians were also philosophers. But there agreement ends. Isocrates believed, or at least Plato says he did, that the rhetorician only needed to know public opinion, not the truth of things, and that writing was an aid to persuasive speech. Socrates, by contrast, argues in this dialogue that a true rhetorician must know the soul of the person addressed, a condition that a written text is unlikely to meet. In the *Phaedrus*, Socrates shows himself to be the true *poietes* who knows how to speak *metrios*.

As the philosopher in the *Symposium* understands how to compose both comedy and tragedy, so in the *Phaedrus* Socrates exemplifies a person who has the ability to deliver a "live" speech filled with soul in the manner of an extemporaneous speaker, to craft it rhythmically and musically in the manner of a *poietes*, and to speak as poets do. As the philosopher in the *Symposium* absorbs and transcends opposing literary genres in his love of wisdom, so in this dialogue Socrates as the true rhetorician commands the verbal skills of opposing rhetorical techniques in the service of philosophy. The true speaker has elements of an *idiotes* and a *poietes*, and something more, speech shaped by philosophical understanding.

C. *Enthousiazo*, Socrates' Possession by a God Within

Early in the dialogue, Socrates with some humor says that he recognizes in Phaedrus "a fellow Bacchic reveler" (228b; cf. 228b and 234d). In more pronounced terms than in any other Platonic work, Socrates speaks of Dionysian possession in the early stages of the dialogue: listening to

---

[38]   Isocrates, "Antidosis" 15.46-47; in "To Philip" 5.27 (346 BCE), he says that when he was young his speeches were "adorned with beautiful rhythmic flow and elaborations" (*kekosmekamen...eurythmiais kai poikiliais*), to make them more pleasing and convincing. In "Antidosis" 15.189, he speaks of captivating an audience not only by what he says but also by the "pleasing harmonies" (*euarmostiais*) of his words.

[39]   Isocrates, "Against the Sophists" 13.17 (composed circa 390 BCE). On Isocrates' style and rhythms, see R. C. Jebb, *The Attic Orators* vol. 2 (London, 1893) 51-75. Alkidamas also speaks about using words "at the right time and musically" (*eukairos kai mousikos*), "On those who write written speeches" 31.

Phaedrus read Lysias' speech, he is caught up in a Bacchic frenzy and is himself in the grip of the god when delivering his first speech (234d, 238d). At this point in the *Phaedrus*, Socrates' divine possession is still imperfect and leads to a wrong-headed account of love (cf. 242c).

But if Socrates' initial Dionysian "enthusiasm" leads him astray, the problem is not in divine possession, per se. Souls which do not have a god within will never sprout wings and be carried heavenward (cf. 249ce). Individuals of mortal and reasoned self-restraint who keep Eros at bay are doomed to roam forever under the earth (cf. 256e-257a). To be a true lover, that is, a true lover of wisdom, divine possession is essential. As seen above, such possession goes beyond philosophic recollection (*anamnesis*) but includes forceful seizure (cf. 250a and 252c). A variety of gods may be identified with the force which takes possession. Dionysos, or at least his Bacchic frenzy, should not be excluded from this number (cf. 253a), but with possession of this sort Dionysos has become a metaphor for possession and not the primary source of divine madness. Because Socrates follows the love of wisdom, he follows in the footsteps of Zeus and dances in his chorus, but we must understand the primary god of possession as Eros himself, the God of Love who seizes and snatches and who turns the lover, guiding him toward philosophy (cf. 257b). In the language of lyric poetry, Eros causes sweat and a fever (251b). He is also an in-flowing of water from the spring and stream of Desire, the flood of which saturates the lover and spills over in its abundance and soaks the beloved (251be, 253a, 255c). The pouring-in causes wings to bud out.

At the end of the palinode, Socrates says that this is a praise of Eros "to the best of my abilities" (257a). Some argue that this signifies that Socrates was not inspired, or if inspired that the source of inspiration came from within. It should be remembered, however, that the poet of the *Odyssey* can say simultaneously that he is "self-taught" and inspired by the Muses and Apollo. To acknowledge one's hand in composition does not exclude the in-flowing of the divine. When talking more calmly with Phaedrus after the palinode, Socrates says of his speeches that he "blames the gods of this place, and maybe the prophets of the Muses as well, the ones singing over our heads who might have breathed this gift into us" (262d).

D. The Frisky Black Horse
(246ab, 248ab, 253c-254e)

In a famous image, Socrates asks Phaedrus to think of the soul as a team of winged horses, one white and the other black, "ruled" by a charioteer. Socrates says nothing about the chariot itself, perhaps to signify that in its pure form the soul is without a body. The two horses are of opposite natures as well as color. The white is in every way beautiful and obedient, while the black one scarcely obeys whip or goad (cf. 246ab, 248ab, 253c-254e). The charioteer treats the black brutally. Some, like D. H. Lawrence's Lady Chatterley, strenuously protest: "Don't you think it's rather cruel, the way Socrates drives his black horse–jerking him back till his mouth and tongue are full of blood, and bruising his haunches? Don't you think one could manage a horse better than that?" Her crippled husband, impotent from a war wound, retorts: "Perhaps not a vicious horse." Critical of her finding Socrates a bully, he asks: "What do you mean exactly by the black horse in this case?" To which his wife replies: "Doesn't it mean the bodily satisfactions? Doesn't it mean the body straining after the goal of its own gratification?" Eventually Lady Chatterley's head will be turned by the gruff gamekeeper of her husband's estate.[40]

It is, of course, a mistake to equate Socrates with the charioteer, but Lady Chatterley has a point. If the black horse were not disobedient, neither the bashful charioteer nor the modest white horse would ever approach the boy, his face "flashing like a lightning bolt" (254b). Even when the beloved has been seen, it requires the unrepentant black horse, its "head down, tail straight back, biting on the bit, shameless" (254d) and still indifferent to the charioteer's whip or its partner's sense of shame, to snarl and drag the reluctant pair forward. Only after it is violently and repeatedly bloodied is the black horse subdued, now "humbled...[and] devastated by fear" (254e) when it sees the beautiful boy. Socrates concludes his tale: "Then at last it actually happens that the lover's soul follows the darling with awe and a sense of shame" (254e). Why does the charioteer treat the black horse so violently?

In the *Symposium* Socrates seems to be more tolerant of physical eros than he is in the *Phaedrus*, acknowledging that it is the essential first step to what may become a transcendent eros. The Socrates of the *Phaedrus* is no less aware that without earthly beauty entering the soul through the eyes there can be no awakening of a transcendent beauty or an itching of wings sprouting anew. But once the lustful lightning flash of the earthly vision is seen, in the *Phaedrus* awe and a sense of shame are felt and the black horse, ugly and arrogant, must be beaten into submission. Sexual desire stimulates what Socrates calls the "unnatural pleasure" to reproduce. For the philosopher, physical beauty causes the pores of the soul to soften and the stalks of its former wings to thrust forward, in an inward journey without sexual outlet, to recall the Forms in the realm beyond the heavens (cf. 250e-251d).[41] But as Lady Chatterley showed, the journey is

---

[40]   Lawrence, *The First Lady Chatterley* (London, 1972) 20-21.

not for everyone.

E. Written texts as play; the myth of Theuth (274d-275b)

As described above (pages 85-86), Theuth, the inventor of letters (along with numbers, calculation, geometry, astronomy, and games of dice), and his king hold differing views regarding the benefit or harm of his invention. The scientist comprehends his invention less fully than his king Thamus (the god Ammon) who understands that writing will only provide an appearance of knowledge rather than real teaching. It is indeed a drug but a drug for reminding rather than for true remembering. The king distinguishes true memory (*anamnesis*), which comes from within and is of essential remembrances, from letters which remind people of what they already know and cause the powers of true recollection to atrophy. Writing, thus, in the king's view offers an appearance of wisdom rather than true wisdom (274c-275b).

Socrates shares similar views. At best, writing is a copy and likeness, a painter's image, of the real thing (275d-276a).[42] Unlike living conversation, possessed with soul, the written word is helpless to answer questions asked of it, unable to defend itself from a passing stranger, having no idea to whom it should speak and to whom it should not. Anyone who writes without knowledge of the truth is nothing more than a mechanical writer, whether he be a poet, or prose writer of speeches, or writer of laws (278d). It is foolish to believe that texts can be left as memorial or manifesto of the self or as a doctrine of the truth (275c). Those who gain confidence from book learning are "difficult to be with" (275b) because they become blind to their own ignorance and forget how to philosophize.[43]

How should this criticism be applied to Plato, a philosopher, and not a god/king like Thamus? Many say Thamus' distrust applies equally to all writing, even if Plato tries to mitigate the failings of the written word by imitating oral speech in his dialogues. But imitation it remains. Others think Plato is being ironic. The work of the philosopher is paradoxical: he

---

[41] Compare Griswold's comment about the art of speaking: "The problem of rhetoric is rooted in the problem of attaining *self-knowledge*. The ingredients of the problem are set out in the palinode's description of the influence of character on thought...Even the soul's inner discourse with itself is an effort of the soul to persuade itself of something, to lead itself from one thought or opinion to another" (note 5; p. 197).

[42] See note 19 and Appendix D.

[43] Griswold (note 5) 206.

seeks the truth which is fixed and stable (like writing), but the love of and search for wisdom is forever evolving (like living speech), a paradoxical union perfectly captured by Plato's invention of the dialogue form. A third view latches on to a phrase that describes spoken dialectic as "written" in the soul (276a; cf. 278a). This metaphoric slip reveals how Plato the writer cannot escape from the language of writing even when he tries to discuss the superiority of the spoken word.[44]

Of the three, the first view appears most helpful, even if Socrates appears to praise writing in ways Thamus does not seem to imagine. For example, when criticizing writing in general, Socrates describes the best speeches—about the just, beautiful and good—as being "written in the soul" for reminding (*hypomnesis*); only these can be "clear, complete, and worthy of seriousness" (278a). Why written in the soul? Does such language undermine Socrates' point, as Derrida claims, or does it suggest that as physical beauty, if handled correctly, is a reminder of its heavenly counterpart, so writing in the soul, if handled correctly, can serve as a *hypomnesis* of true recollection? Speeches written in the soul "bear seed" and, when planted in other fields, make those seeds forever immortal and "the person possessing them [to be] as happy as is humanly possible" (276e-277a).[45]

We should not assume that Socrates and King Thamus speak for Plato fully. The written dialogue form which Plato invents invites reflection and engagement more than unquestioning confidence. The dialogue's imitation of living voices set in a time and place mirrors the philosopher's search for truth through dialectical cross-examination. It also mixes philosophy with myth, human drama, friendship and erotic playfulness. In its multiple parts, the *Phaedrus*, like other Platonic dialogues, reflects the on-going drama of human struggle and choice, exposing the likely dangers and rewards of the choices made. In the end, it is not possible to say what the dialogue is *about*, that the head is finally one thing or another. And perhaps it does not matter. The dialogue is drama, an experience of truth in action that does not depend on arguments, though it may include them.

---

[44]   For the first view, see Hackforth (note 5) 162-64 and Ferrari (note 4) 204-22; for the second view, see Burger (note 5) 108-9; for the third view, see Jacques Derrida, *La dissémination* (Paris, 1972) 69-198. Against Derrida, see Griswold (note 5) 230-41 and more broadly about the Platonic dialogue and writing, 202-29, as well as White (note 6) 229-91. On the dialogue form and types of irony in it, see Charles Griswold, "Irony in the Platonic Dialogues," *Philosophy and Literature* 26 (2002) 84-106.

[45]   Compare Plato's Seventh Letter 341c-d: political knowledge, he writes, cannot be put into words but, "after a prolonged intercourse between a teacher and his pupil, in pursuit of this subject, like a light flashing from a fire just kindled, it is born in the soul and straightway nourishes itself."

As readers we are challenged to participate in that human story, the mythic visions, and dialectic questioning for understanding. If, like all texts, the written dialogue is lifeless and devoid of soul, our engagement with it may be said to endow the written word with life. With Lady Chatterley we may object to "Socrates'" (or, more appropriately, to the charioteer's) poor management of the frisky black horse, but the dialogue draws us in as it drew in Lady Chatterley, so that, like her, we respond to the written words with living speech. Wild, provocative, mysterious, the *Phaedrus* engenders still, after two millennia, a conversation of passionate dissent and sympathy in which it appears that true philosophy—as demonstrated by Socrates—is a form of action. If the *Phaedrus* is to be compared to a body, it is a body in motion with the energy and excitement of the black horse disciplined by philosophic restraint.

APPENDIX A: SAPPHO AND ANACREON

At 235b-c, Socrates mentions some old and wise men and women—and he has in mind the beautiful Sappho or the wise Anacreon or even some prose writers—who would scold him if he did not contest Phaedrus' praise of Lysias' speech. The Greeks considered Sappho and Anacreon as the supreme examples of early love poetry. A sample of their poetry is included here. All translations in the appendices are my own.

Sappho, born on the island of Lesbos in the second half of the 7th century, was celebrated by the Greeks as the tenth Muse. Of her nine books of poems, only fragments survive, whether from papyri rolls found in Egypt or from quotations in ancient authors. Fragments are numbered from D. Campbell, *Greek Lyric* vol. I (Cambridge, Mass., 1982), the Loeb Classical Library.

fr. 16 Some men say that a host of cavalry, others a host
of infantry, and others a host of ships are the most beautiful
on the black earth. But I say that it is
whatever someone loves.

It's not hard for all to understand;
for she who far surpasses all
mankind in beauty, Helen, left
her noble husband

and went to Troy, sailing, with no
thought of child or dear parents,
but [love] led her away ...
...

...
...   nimbly   ...
...and now reminded me of Anactoria
who is not here;

I would prefer to see her lovely gait
and the shining gleam of her face
than the Lydian chariots and foot soldiers
in their armor.
...

fr. 31. He seems to me equal to a god
that man who sits opposite you
and listens close up to your
sweet voice

and lovely laughter, which causes
my heart in my chest to tremble. When I
look briefly, it is no longer possible
for me to speak,

but my tongue [freezes] in silence,
a slender flame immediately races
beneath my flesh, with my eyes I see nothing,
my ears hum,

sweat pours down me, trembling
takes hold all over, I am paler
than grass, and seem to myself
just short of death.

But endure all, since...

fr. 37. ...in my [grief] dripping...
...
may winds and anxieties carry off that man
who rebukes me...

fr. 42. their passion has chilled,
and they slacken their wings.

fr. 47. Love shook my thoughts,
as a wind falling on mountain oak trees.

fr. 48. You came, and I yearned for you,
        but you cooled my heart on fire with desire.

fr. 130. Love once again limb-loosening spins me about
        the bitter-sweet, unconquerable beast.

   Anacreon, circa 570-circa 485 BCE, is from Teos in Asia Minor but moved to Abdera in Thrace (circa 545 BCE) as the Persians threatened the Ionian coastal cities. He later moved to the court of Polycrates, tyrant of Samos, the most illustrious of the Greeks in his day. Tradition has it that he and Polycrates were rivals for the same Thracian boy. When Polycrates was murdered in 522, Anacreon was called to the court of Hippias, tyrant of Athens (527-510 BCE) and may have died there in the early years of the democracy. He composed in many meters and is thought to have greatly influenced the young Aeschylus in his own metrical schemas, although there is no evidence that Anacreon himself wrote tragedy. From the limited range of what survives, a graceful style is evident and repeated attention to wine, Dionysus, old age, and love (both homosexual and heterosexual in orientation). Fragments are numbered from Campbell, *Greek Lyric* vol. II (Cambridge, Mass., 1988), the Loeb Classical Library.

fr. 359. I love Kleoboulos,
        I am mad about Kleoboulos,
        I gaze on Kleoboulos.

fr. 360. Boy with the glance of a young maiden,
        I seek you out but you do not notice,
        Unaware that you are the charioteer
        Of my soul.

fr. 376. Mounting and poising myself once again
        from the Leucadian rock I plunge into the gray sea, drunk with love.
           [To leap from the high cliffs at the southern tip of White Island was said to be a cure for love. Sappho is reported to have hurled herself from these cliffs to cure herself of her love for Phaon ("Bright light").]

fr. 396. Bring water, bring wine, my boy, bring us a crown
        of flowers. Get them so I may box against Love.

fr. 398. Love's dice are
        madness and battle-clamor.

fr. 413. Love once again like a smith has clobbered me
with a great hammer and drenched me in a chilling stream.

fr. 417. Thracian filly, why do you
look at me with that shy sideways glance,
pitilessly fleeing me? Do you suppose
I have no skill? Know that I could
neatly snare you with a bridle,
and with rein in hand wheel
you 'round the racecourse post.
But now you feed in the meadows
and play, bounding at ease,
since you have no dexterous horseman
to be your trainer.

fr. 428. I love once again and I do not love
and I am mad and am not mad.

fr. 446. crazed hot-patch
[of women]

fr. 450. drinking Love

fr. 459. melting Love

fr. 460. Love's freight
[Europa on the bull's back]

fr. 505d. I long to sing of graceful-moving
Love, his head luxuriously
garlanded with a flowery band.
He is the master of the gods;
he overpowers mortals.

APPENDIX B: IBYCUS

At 242b-d, Socrates is visited by his daimon who warns him not to cross the river before he purifies himself, as if he had committed an offense against the divine. Pondering what it might be, Socrates remembers the words of Ibycus "bringing harm upon the gods, I win honor among men," and then realizes his offense.

Ibycus, Sappho's contemporary, from Rhegium in southern Italy, traveled widely, much in demand for his choral poetry. He is particularly known for his love poetry, as seen from Cicero's *Tusculan Disputations* (4.71): "Anacreon's poetry is completely erotic. More than all others, Ibycus of Rhegium burnt with love, as his writings show. We see that for these men love is lustful." Fragments are numbered from Campbell, *Greek Lyric* vol. III (Cambridge, Mass., 1991), the Loeb Classical Library.

fr. 287. Love once again looking at me with melting eyes
     under his dark-blue eyelids
hurls me with spells of all kinds
     into the boundless nets of Aphrodite.
How I tremble at his approach,
just as a prize-winning horse still wearing its yoke
into old age enters the contest unwilling with his swift chariot.

fr. 286. In the springtime, the Cydonian
apple-trees bloom, watered by
running rivers where the garden
of the Maidens stands inviolate,
as the vine-blossoms burst in bloom
under the shading vine shoots. But for me
     love is never at rest in any season;

but like the Thracian North Wind blazing
with lightning it darts dark and fearless from Aphrodite's
home, with parching fits of madness,
   setting my thoughts fiercely aquiver
from the ground up.

fr. 288. Euryalus, offshoot of the blue-eyed Graces,
       delight of the lovely-haired Seasons, you
       Aphrodite and soft-eyed Persua-
          sion nursed among the rose blossoms.

["Persuasion" is a cult title of Aphrodite at Pharsalus and in
Lesbos, whereas at Sicyon she was connected with Apollo and
Artemis and at Argos exclusively with Artemis. At Athens, the cult
of Persuasion was housed in the temple of Aphrodite Pandemos
and her priestess was awarded a special seat in the Theater of
Dionysos. In Hesiod, she is the daughter of Ocean and Tethys, but
in Sappho she is Aphrodite's daughter.]

Phallus-Bird

Birds with phallus-bodies are not uncommon in this period. Most phalloi-birds, but not all, have an eye and sometimes a mouth on the tip of the phallus. In some instances, a naked lady is depicted riding the bird.

Athenian Red-Figure, circa 470 BCE. Two-handled cup (skyphos). Courtesy of Museum of Fine Arts, Boston. RES .08.31 C. Gift of E. P. Warren

Winged Phalloi

Facing sphinx-like phalloi, each winged with an animal haunch, legs, and tail. The inscription between the phalloi reads TOUTO EMOI / KAI TOUTO SOI ("This for me / and this for you"). Both image and inscription suggest symmetry and equality.

Relief Sculpture, House of the Phourne. Delos. From the Hellenistic period. Courtesy of École Français D'Athènes.

APPENDIX C: WINGED EROS

At 252b, Socrates says that human beings call the passion which they have been discussing winged Love (*Eros potenos*) but that the gods call him Winged (*Pteros*), a name which Socrates suspects will cause the boy (to whom the palinode is addressed) to laugh because of his youth. Socrates has learned the language of the gods from two "unpublished" Homeric verses, one of which is outrageous (*hybristikon*) and not entirely metrical: "but the gods call him Winged, because he makes things rise." "He makes things rise" translates *pterophytor' ananken,* literally "wing-making compulsion" (for this version, I thank my student Collomia Charles). Gods' language draws on Greek slang which calls the aroused penis Winged (what in English might be rendered a Winged Pecker or Cock) as is seen in Greek art where a stiff penis is often depicted as the neck and head of a bird with outstretched wings. This association is best discussed by William Arrowsmith, "Aristophanes' *Birds*: The Fantasy Politics of Eros," *Arion* n.s.1 (1973) 119-67, esp. Appendix II on the *Phaedrus*, pp. 164-67. As Arrowsmith observes, Socrates' speech is filled with double entendres, describing a soul as swelling, pulsing, throbbing, and sweating as its wings begin to grow. The use of the phrase *ho tou pterou kaulos*, "the wing's stalk" at 251b6 does much to confirm Arrowsmith's insight. *Kaulos* is used only here in Plato's *oeuvre*; it refers principally to the stalk of a plant and metaphorically, in the medical writers, to the duct of a penis, a woman's cervix, or the penis itself. No doubt, it is the gods' use of slang which causes the youth to laugh.

APPENDIX D:
EXTEMPORANEOUS SPEECH AS ALIVE
AND ENSOULED; *POIĒTĒS LOGŌN*

After Socrates compares *written* speech at 275d to painting (*zographia*) (painting appears to be alive, but it remains in complete silence when questioned and is unable to defend itself), he turns his attention to praise extempore speech, the legitimate brother of the bastard sibling, written speech. Then, in a phrase which has caused much confusion, Socrates describes improvised speech as "*written* with knowledge in the soul *of one who understands.*" I discuss in the Interpretive Essay why it should be written at all (page 98). Socrates goes on to praise extempore speech for its ability to defend itself, an argument which Phaedrus has no difficulty in understanding: "You are referring to the speech of a person *who knows*, a speech *living and ensouled* (*zos kai empsykhos*), the written version of whicih would justly (*dikaios*) be called an *image* (*eidolon*)." Phaedrus' metaphoric language is all the more striking as it closely parallels the metaphors for extempore speech in a treatise written at the time of the *Phaedrus* by a rhetorician named Alkidamas. He, like Plato, is defending the value of extemporaneous speech-making against the rising tide of professional speech writers. It would be nice to know which text came first, but in a certain sense it does not matter greatly. Whether Plato borrowed from Alkidamas, or vice-versa, Plato took the argument much further than Alkidamas does in his treatise. Alkidamas' polemic makes clear that at the time Plato was writing the *Phaedrus*, a debate was raging in Athens between a new school of writers, which included Isocrates, and traditional orators. Both sides of the debate called the writer of written speeches a *poietes logon*, "a maker or crafter of speeches," while the extemporaneous speaker, judging from Alkidamas, called himself simply a *rhetor*, or orator. Considered from the point of view of this debate, one might suspect that Plato's use of *poietes* for Lysias (circa 410 BCE) evoked, obliquely and anachronistically, for Plato's contemporaries circa 360 BCE a short-hand reference for *poietes logon*, as if Lysias' written prose were a stand-in for Isocrates and other fourth-century speech writers. For Isocrates, *poietes* had a double sense, both "skilled craftsman" and "poet," as he prided himself for composing "rhythmically and musically" "with rather poetic and elaborate phrasing" and "pleasing harmonies."[1] Socrates absorbs elements from both sides of the debate: his criticisms parallel Alkidamas' against written speech (although Socrates calls himself an *idiotes*), but like a *poietes* he speaks *metrios*, "with measure." He further separates himself from both by insisting that all speakers must speak with prior knowledge about their subject and about the souls of those receiving the speech.

Alkidamas, born in Elaia near Pergamon in Asia Minor, came to Athens where he studied with Gorgias, as did his rival Isocrates; in time, he is said to have become the head of Gorgias' "school." What follows are excerpts from Alkidamas' "On those who write written speeches" (sections 27-28 and 33-34, respectively) [2]

(27) I do not think it is right (*dikaion*) that written speeches should be called speeches; rather they should be considered *images* (*eidola*) and appearances and imitations of speeches. And in a similar manner we could hold the same opinion of them as we do of bronze statues and of stone images and of *drawn images* (*gegrammena zoa*). For just as these are imitations of real bodies and offer delight in viewing, they provide no use for our lives. (28) In the same way, written speech (*gegrammenos logos*) has a single appearance and a single arrangement and offers certain astonishing effects when viewed from a book but, because it is immobile at the opportune moment, it provides no benefit for those who use it. Just as real bodies offer a far inferior symmetry compared to that of beautiful statues but provide many more benefits for work, so also a speech which is uttered straight from one's thinking on the spur of the moment *is ensouled and lives* (*empsukhos esti kai ze*) and follows upon the unfolding events and is similar to real bodies, but the written speech, while similar in nature to the image of speech, does not share in its immense vigor.

---

[1]   Isocrates, "Against the Sophists" 16, "Antidosis" 47 and 189, respectively.

[2]   For a text and a translation, see J. V. Muir, *Alcidamas. The Works and Fragments* (London, 2001). Muir believes, unlike some, that Alkidamas "took his ideas and philosophy either from a reading of the *Phaedrus* or directly from Socrates himself" (p. 62). The translation here is my own.

...

(33) Yet even so one shouldn't believe that we prefer the ability to extemporize over the art of writing when we exhort people to speak "at random." For we think that orators (*rhetores*) must plan their thoughts in advance and arrange the order of their speech in advance but when it comes to the order of their words they must extemporize. For the benefit which the precision of scripted speeches provides is not so great as is the appropriateness of the occasion for directing the words spoken on the spur of the moment. (34) Therefore, the person who desires to be a powerful (*deinos*) orator, and not just an adequate *craftsman of speeches* (*poietes logon*), and who prefers to make fine use of the moment rather than to utter words and phrases with precision, and who is serious about gaining the good will of the audience as his ally rather than having their malice against him, and who wishes in addition to have a relaxed frame of mind and a ready *memory* (*mnene*) with no detectable *forgetfulness* (*lethe*), and who is eager to acquire the power to make speeches which corresponds to the needs of life, wouldn't such a person, if he always and on every circumstance gave thoughtful rehearsal *to extempore speaking* and regarded writing *as play* and a subordinate activity, be suitably judged by people of good judgment to be himself a person of good judgment?

APPENDIX E:
ECHOES OF THE PALINODE: SHAKESPEARE, DONNE, WORDSWORTH, ELIOT

After Marsilio Ficino's celebrated *Theologia Platonica*, completed in 1474, his *Five Keys of Platonic Wisdom* in 1477, and his translation of the complete works of Plato into Latin in 1484 (Florence; 2nd ed., Venice, 1491),[1] the themes and ideas of the *Phaedrus* began to percolate throughout Europe. For example:

William Shakespeare's *A Midsummer Night's Dream* (circa 1600 CE), At the beginning of Act V, Scene I, Hippolyta and Theseus discuss the play within the play. Theseus' analogy between madman, lover, and poet offers a hymn to the imagination which in its celebration of "the forms of things unknown" suggests echoes of Socrates' palinode. One wonders if the play itself, set outside Athens in the green wood where conventional attachments are suspended temporarily and human beings are open to otherworldly spirits and erotic inspirations before they return to the city, is not itself influenced by the *Phaedrus*:

HIPPOLYTA

Tis strange, my Theseus, that these lovers speak of.

THESEUS

More strange than true. I never may believe
These antic fables nor these fairy toys.
Lovers and madman have such seething brains,

---

[1]   Cf. Michael J. B. Allen, *The Platonism of Marsilio Ficino: A Study of his Phaedrus Commentary, Its Sources and Genesis* (Berkeley, 1984).

Such shaping fantasies, that apprehend
More than cool reason ever comprehends.
The lunatic, the lover, and the poet
Are of imagination all compact.
One sees more devils than vast hell can hold:
That is the madman. The lover, all as frantic,
Sees Helen's beauty in a brow of Egypt.
The poet's eye, in a fine frenzy rolling,
Doth glance from heaven to earth, from earth to heaven;
And as imagination bodies forth
The forms of things unknown, the poet's pen
Turns them to shapes, and gives to airy nothing
A local habitation and a name.
Such tricks hath strong imagination
That, if it would but apprehend some joy,
It comprehends some bringer of that joy;
Or in the night, imagining some fear,
How easy is a bush supposed a bear!

Shakespeare's Sonnets (the collected Sonnets first published by Thomas Thorpe, 1609). In their surges of realistic and contradictory emotions, the Sonnets tend to resist Christian NeoPlatonism even as NeoPlatonic idealism exerts a continuous pressure upon the poems. If, as some argue,[2] the Fair Young Man and the Dark Lady of the Sonnets are not read as real personages, but as figures representing an inner torment between good and bad love, then Socrates' account of the white and black horses of the soul in the *Phaedrus* may be thought to have aided, whether directly or not, the Renaissance poet's abstraction of the spiritual battle of good and bad love within the self. If so, Shakespeare turned the conflict into a Pauline battle, making the good angel male and a friend, and the bad angel female and erotic, as in Sonnet 144 (first published in *The Passionate Pilgrim*, 1599).

Two loves I have, of comfort and despair,
Which like two spirits do suggest me still:
The better angel is a man right fair,
The worser spirit a woman colored ill.
To win me soon to hell, my female evil
Tempteth my better angel from my side,
And would corrupt my saint to be a devil,
Wooing his purity with her foul pride.
And whether that my angel be turned fiend

---

[2]   Cf. Barbara Everett, "Good and bad loves: Shakespeare, Plato and the plotting of the Sonnets," *Times Literary Supplement* July 5, 2002, 13-5.

Suspect I may, yet not directly tell;
But being both from me, both to each friend,
I guess one angel in another's hell.
    Yet this shall I ne'er know, but live in doubt,
    Till my bad angel fire my good one out.

John Donne's "The Extasie," written between the 1590s and 1617 but not published until 1631,[1] takes a distinctly anti-Platonic, and perhaps specially an anti-Phaidrean, stance, teasing the beloved with a neo-Platonic theory of love (" When love.../ interinanimates two soules") as a prelude to a physical seduction ("to'our bodies turne wee then"). The quotation begins from line 33:

But as all severall soules containe
    Mixture of things, they know not what,
Love, these mixt soules, doth mixe againe,
    And makes both one, each this and that.
A single violet transplant,
    The strength, the colour, and the size,
(All which before was poore, and scant,)
    redoubles still, and multiples.
When love, with one another so
    Interinanimates two soules,
That abler soule, which thence doth flow,
    Defects of lonelinesse controules.
Wee then, who are this new soule, know,
    Of what we are compos'd, and made,
For, th'Atomies of which we grow,
    Are soules, whom no change can invade.
But O alas, so long, so farre
    Our bodies why doe wee forbeare?
They are ours, though they are not wee, Wee are
    The intelligences, they the spheares.
We owe them thankes, because they thus,
    Did us, to us, at first convay,
Yeelded their forces, sense to us,
    Nor are drosse to us, but allay.
On man heavens influence workes not so,
    But that it first imprints the ayre,

---

[3]   Cf. Frank Warnke (ed.), *John Donne: Poetry and Prose* (New York, 1967) 43: "The title ["Extasie"] has reference to the mystical state in which the soul, temporarily separated from the body, is vouchsafed a direct experience of divine truth, the so-called *beatific vision*" (his italics).

Soe soule into the soule may flow
   Though it to body first repaire.
As our blood labours to beget
   Spirits, as like soules as it can,
Because such fingers need to knit
   That subtile knot, which makes us man:
So must pure lovers soules descend
   T'affections, and to faculties,
Which sense may reach and apprehend,
   Else a great Prince in prison lies.
To'our bodies turne wee then, that so
   Weake men on love reveal'd may looke;
Loves mysteries in soules doe grow,
   But yet the body is his booke.
And if some lover, such as wee,
   Have heard this dialogue of one,
Let him still marke us, he shall see
   Small change, when we'are to bodies gone.

William Wordsworth's "Intimations of Immortality from Recollections of Early Childhood," published 1807, engages with Socrates' palinode very differently from Shakespeare and Donne. In this poem, memory of the soul's descent into a mortal body fades as the child matures, a much more melancholic view than that found in Plato and one stripped of any suggestion of the revitalizing powers of Eros. Wordsworth's consolation for the lost unity of the soul and the visionary gleam of childhood comes not in the form of sexual Eros but of sympathy and a reflective love of nature. I first quote section V of this poem of eleven sections and then pick up in the middle of section X.

V

Our birth is but a sleep and a forgetting:
The Soul that rises with us, our life's Star,
   Hath had elsewhere its setting,
     And cometh from afar:
     Not in entire forgetfulness,
     And not in utter nakedness,
But trailing clouds of glory do we come
     From God, who is our home:
Heaven lies about us in our infancy!

Shades of the prison-house begin to close
    Upon the growing Boy
But He beholds the light, and whence it flows,
    He sees it in his joy;
The Youth, who daily farther from the east
    Must travel, still is Nature's Priest,
    And by the vision splendid
    Is on his way attended;
At length the Man perceives it die away,
And fade into the light of common day.

...

        X

...

    We will grieve not, rather find
    Strength in what remains behind;
    In the primal sympathy
    Which having been must ever be;
    In the soothing thoughts that spring
    Out of human suffering;
    In the faith that looks through death,
In years that bring the philosophic mind.

       XI
And O, ye Fountains, Meadows, Hills, Groves,
Forebode not any severing of our loves!
Yet in my heart of hearts I feel your might;
I only have relinquished one delight
To live beneath your more habitual sway.
I love the Brooks which down their channels fret,
Even more than when I tripped lightly as they;
The innocent brightness of a new-born Day
    Is lovely yet;
The Clouds that gather round the setting sun
Do take a sober colouring from an eye
That hath kept watch o'er man's mortality;
Another race hath been, and other palms are won.
Thanks to the human heart by which we live,
Thanks to its tenderness, its joys, and fears,
To me the meanest flower that blows can give
Thoughts that do often lie too deep for tears.

T. S. Eliot's "Lune de Miel", published 1920, is perhaps the most directly engaged with the palinode. The American couple, traveling to Europe for their honeymoon, find themselves on a summer night in Ravenna, having journeyed from the Pays-Bas (The LowLands) en route to Terre Haute (Highland), Indiana, After a night in a sleazy hotel, they wake in the morning scratching and swollen with bites, the modern equivalent for these young lovers of the itching of the wings which a true lover of beauty would experience. But this groom has a miserly, economizing soul, one "diluted by mortal moderation," as Socrates would say. One imagines that he will never reach the philosopher's Terre Haute nor help his beloved do the same.[4]

LUNE DE MIEL

Ils ont vu les Pays-Bas, ils rentrent à Terre Haute;
Mais une nuit d'été, les voici à Ravenne,
A l'aise entre deux draps, chez deux centaines de punaises;
La sueur aestivale, et une forte odeur de chienne.
Ils restent sur le dos écartant les genoux
De quatre jambs molles tout gonflées de morsures.
On relève le drap pour mieux égratigner.
Moins d'une lieue d'ici est Saint Apollinaire
En Classe, basilique connue des amateurs
De chapitaux d'acanthe que tournoie le vent.

  Ils vont prendre le train de huit heures
Prolonger leurs misères de Padoue à Milan
Où se trouvent la Cène, et un restaurant pas cher.
Lui pense aux pourboires, et rédige son bilan.
Ils auront vu la Suisse et traversé la France.
Et Saint Apollinaire, raide et ascetique,
Vieille usine désaffectée de Dieu, tient encore
Dans ses pierres écroulantes la forme précise de Byzance.

---

[4]   For a study of this poem, infused with Ruskin, Dante, and St. Augustine as much as with the *Phaedrus*, see William Arrowsmith, "Eros in Terre Haute: T. S. Eliot's 'Lune de Miel,'" *The New Criterion* 1 (1982) 22-41, esp. 31-8. A poet, as Eliot wrote in "Tradition and the Individual Talent" (1919), must have "historical sense [which] compels a man to write not merely with his own generation in his bones, but with a feeling that the whole of the literature of Europe from Homer…has a simultaneous existence and composes a simultaneous order."

HONEYMOON (a literal translation)

They have seen the LowLands, they are going back to the HighLand;
But one summer night, here they are in Ravenna,
Lounging between two sheets, with two hundred bed-bugs;
Summer sweat, and a strong odor of bitch.
They lie on their backs opening their knees
Of four soft legs all swollen with bites.
They lift up the sheet to scratch better.
Less than a league from here is Saint Apollinaire
En Classe, a basilica known to amateurs
Of acanthus capitals which the wind turns.

  They are going to take the eight o'clock train
To prolong their miseries from Padua to Milan
Where they'll find the Last Supper, and a cheap restaurant.
He thinks about tips, and works out his accounts.
They will have seen Switzerland and crossed France.
And Saint Apollinaire, stiff and ascetic,
Old factory vacated by God, keeps still
In its crumbling stones the precise form of Byzantine.

GLOSSARY

To Adore, see *To love*.

Arrangement (*diathesis*), **discovery** (*heuresis*), and **recollection** (*anamnesis*).

Rhetorical show pieces were conventionally judged according to arrangement (i.e., the clever arrangement of traditional material) and discovery, or invention (i.e., the use of novel matter), the former being considered the more important of the two, if we can follow Isocrates' judgment (cf. *Helen* 11-13). Socrates and Phaedrus agree that Lysias' speech should be evaluated according to arrangement, not discovery, and Socrates in his first speech is clearly more concerned with arrangement than discovery (cf. 237b-238c). At the end of the dialogue (278c-d) Socrates uses a different word for arranging (*syntithemai*), perhaps because he can apply the less marked word to a wide range of genres and compositions.

If arrangement is more valued than discovery in terms of composition, from a philosophic perspective the reverse is true. True rhetoric requires discovery, or more accurately re-discovery or *recollection* of the *Forms* through *dialectic*. In this sense, discovery describes rediscovering something which has always been there but which has been forgotten. Arrangement without discovery of this kind is, like Lysias' speech or Socrates' first speech, merely clever. In the second half of this dialogue, when Socrates and Phaedrus refer to "masters" who have discovered or found various rhetorical components, reference to discovery or finding is frequently ironic, but at 269c Socrates says that rhetorical art cannot be discovered unless someone *first* knows how to think dialectically. Here, he is not being ironic. In one of numerous verbal echoes linking the palinode to the discussion of rhetoric which follows, the verb "to have discovered" 269c recalls the same verb describing the lover who finds a beloved suitable to his soul (cf. 252e and 253b).

Art (*techne*), **skill** (*sophos*)

Techne refers to a skill, discipline, craft, or trade such as medicine, horse-raising, farming, sculpting, which is teachable and capable of being passed on from one generation to the next. It requires a combination of what we would call art and science to master. An *idiotes* refers to a person who lacks a particular skill in question or all skills; in this context, the opposite of an *idiotes* is a *tekhnites* or *tekhnikos*, an "artistic" or "skilful" person (used throughout the second half of the dialogue, including in the superlative to refer to Theuth at 274e where I translate it as "the greatest of technicians").

In its earliest usage, the adjective *sophos* describes a person who has mastered a craft; only near the end of the fifth century does it describe someone who is *wise*, or proficient and skilled in thought and the imparting of knowledge. When Socrates calls Thrasymachos and others *sophoi* or skilled masters in the art of speaking at 266c, he implies the possible common ground between the *philo-sophos* and the *sophos* rhetorician. Also see *Unskilled speaker*.

To be fond of, see *To love*.

Beloved, see *Lover*.

Boy, see *Lover*.

Cicadas

The cicadas, as Socrates tells the story, were once human, born before the Muses. Upon hearing the Muses sing, they gave themselves completely to song, singing without food or drink until they slipped unaware into death (259b-c). Reborn as creatures exclusively devoted to music, they neither eat nor drink but sing continuously until they die. Then they report back to the Muses, announcing which mortals on earth honor which Muses in particular. If a person has gone through life loving wisdom and honoring heavenly music, the cicadas report to Kalliope (Beautiful-voice) and to Ourania (Heavenly), the two oldest of the Muses and the ones with the sweetest voices.

The cicadas also have a dangerous side; like the Sirens, they can cause mortals to lose their way. In order to escape this bewitching music, Socrates realizes that he and Phaedrus must close their ears to it and concentrate upon philosophical discourse. Ferrari (1987) concentrates on this danger alone, making little of the "gift of honor" (*geras*) that the cicadas offer to those who devote their lives to philosophy and who honor heavenly music. Both powers of the cicadas need to be remembered. The cicadas are like a *pharmakon*, (see below), which has the capacity to help or harm those exposed to it. Like the grove and the hour—noon-time on a hot summer day when most people sleep (259a)—they are conduits allowing passage between realms. There is danger in such travel, as seen in the example of the cicadas themselves who in their love of heavenly music forgot their mortal need for food and drink, and who can cause those lazy of mind to drift off into a noontime slumber. But they also represent opportunity. As Odysseus was able to hear the Sirens' song and sail past, Socrates has both been opened to a vision of the divine and, with Phaedrus' help, has been able to sail past, turning from ecstatic vision to dialectic and to rhetorical and philosophical questions in the second half of the dialogue. The cicadas are also of special interest to Socrates and Phaedrus, as Kalliope and Ourania preside over discourse, both human and divine. Also see *Drug* and *Grove.*

Collection, see *Division.*

Darling, see *Lover.*

Dialectic (*dialektikos*)

Dialectic is a *techne* (see *Art*) which describes the philosophic inquiry or conversation which subjects a premise or definition to cross-examination and review. Aristotle says that Zeno of Elea invented the technique, as he explored how a hypothesis could lead to contradictory conclusions. Socrates introduces the practice of cross-examination (*elenchos*) whereby others question a proposed definition. Socrates' pupil, Plato, may have coined the term dialectic and may have been the one to identify this form of inquiry as a *techne*. In addition to cross-examination, it involves *collection* of parts into a genus and *division* of the whole into species. For Plato, it is the only true form of philosophical inquiry: necessarily an oral exchange, and ideally between two people (cf. *Republic* VII.531-39). His written dialogues offer a copy or approximation of its true form. The adjective is used three times in the *Phaedrus*: 266c (twice) and 276e. The verb *dialegein*, "to have converse with," appears at 232a, 241a, 242a, 259a (twice). Also see *Division.*

Discovery, see *Arrangement.*

Discursive thinking, see *Thinking.*

Divine possession

In his *Theologia Platonica*, the Neoplatonist Proclus (circa 410-485 CE) felt that Socrates is inspired throughout the dialogue from the time he enters the grove: "Having been enraptured by the inspiration that comes from the Nymphs, and having exchanged the activity of the intelligence (*nous*) for divine madness, Socrates propounded a great number of secret doctrines throughout the dialogue. For his mouth was divinely inspired...and everything he taught there was taught in a divinely inspired manner (as he explicitly notes himself). In fact, he makes the local or country divinities responsible for his madness" (vol. I.4) [Proclus, quoted by Michael Allen (1984) 3, in his reference to the Renaissance Platonist Ficino who shares Proclus' view that Socrates is divinely inspired throughout his stay in the grove.] Others feel that Socrates rids himself of his frenzied state before he delivers his second speech (see the Interpretative Essay, page 95).

The language of divine possession appears for the first time in the dialogue even before Socrates leaves the city, when he imagines that Phaedrus sees him as a **synkorybantios**, literally "one joined in Korybantic frenzy or revels" (228b), or (as I translate it) "a fellow bacchic reveler," the two of them sent into a frenzy at the very idea of listening to speeches. Socrates is referring to ecstatic mysteries from the East associated with the goddess Cybele and Dionysos. When Socrates is first in the grove, Dionysos is the central figure identified with divine frenzy: Socrates says that he has been "caught up in a Bacchic frenzy along with" Phaedrus as he listens to Phaedrus read (**synebakcheusa**, 234d). This compound with the verb is extremely rare, as it happens, found only here in Plato's writing; the most striking use of this verb occurs in Euripides' *Bacchae* (726-27) to describe the animate and inanimate world, the maenads on the mountain, the wild animals, and the mountain itself, caught up in the spirit of the god, where its connotations far exceed anything implied here. As if to underline the state of his possession, Socrates addresses Phaedrus here as a "divine source (head)."

Socrates feels no less possessed while delivering his first speech. He calls upon the Muses for inspiration as he begins (237a). Midway through the speech, he interrupts himself and observes that he is not far from speaking in **dithyrambs**, a lyric form again associated with Dionysos (238d; cf. 241e), but he also begins to feel that the divinities of the grove are taking possession of him: he turns to Phaedrus and tells him not to be astonished if he finds Socrates becoming **nympholeptos**, "nymph-possessed," the word that Proclus so admired and found only here in Plato (238d).

But at this point in the dialogue, nymph-possession and Dionysian frenzy do not prevent Socrates from sinning against the god of Love. Influenced partly by Lysias, partly by Dionysos, he gives a wrong-headed and shameful account of love, a speech which he comes to realize is a violation "against the divine" (242c). In his correcting speech which follows, Socrates describes poetic madness as "filling-the-spirit-utterly-with-Bacchos" (**ekbakcheuousa** 245a, a verb used only one other time by Plato), but he also recognizes that there is a higher form of madness than bacchic possession (244a-245a). Some scholars claim that Socrates is in full possession of himself while delivering the palinode, and offer 257a3 to support this view. The vision of the heavens is the reward of those divinely possessed by love, and Socrates seems so rewarded.

The key verb is **enthousiazo**, "to have the god within," "to be enthused," "to be possessed or inspired." It first appears in a rather negative context to describe the engodded Socrates delivering his misguided speech, but the verb is even more prominent in the palinode. The souls of those not enthused will never sprout wings (249c-e). Those who keep Eros at bay live a tempered, self-controlled existence of mortal small-mindedness and, at death, are doomed forever to roam under the earth (256e-257a).

A variety of gods may be identified with this enthusiasm. While Dionysos should not be excluded from this number (cf. 253a), he has become something of a metaphor for possession and not the primary source. The primary god of possession is, of course, Eros himself who seizes (252c) and turns the lover, guiding him toward philosophy (257b). Griswold (1986) (p. 75) suggests that "divine erotic madness is not so much sent from the gods external to the individual as sparked from a source within him, as is suggested by its association with **anamnesis**," but Socrates stresses in the palinode that lovers are invaded by divine "enthusiasm" from without.

Related to the image of enthusiasm is **eudaimonia**, "being in possession of a good daimon or spirit," a word found in its adjectival, nominal, and verbal forms especially within the palinode to describe the "blissful journey" (256d), "blessed lovers" (253c), "blessed chorus-dances" (250b), "blessed visions" (250c), and the "race of the happy gods" (247a). Related is **makarios** to describe blessed harmony (256a), blessed vistas (247a), the blest (250b and 250c). Both words are found especially in the context of initiation at 250b-c and 256a-d. But the blessed state also hovers over those people who use the dialectical art and select the appropriate souls, when sowing and planting their speeches with knowledge (276e-277a). And, of course, Socrates uses "blessed" as a form of address when speaking to Phaedrus (236d and 241e). Also see *Initiation*.

Division (*diairesis*), collection (*sunagoge*)

See *Dialectic*; also note 119 in the Translation, and the Interpretative Essay, page 88-9.

Drug (*pharmakon*), Pharmakeia, speeches (*logoi*), and writing

The Greeks were particularly sensitive to the fact that a drug could be beneficial or harmful, a medicine or a poison. In the *Phaedrus*, Socrates describes himself as "sick with desire to hear speeches" (228b), and says to Phaedrus that he has found the drug, i.e., reading Lysias' speech, which could take him out of the city (230d). But far from being cured of his illness when he has heard the speech, Socrates feels a swelling in his chest to compose one of his own (235c-d). Near the grove where Socrates and Phaedrus lie on the grass delivering speeches, the nymph Oreithuia was thrown from a rock and killed by the North Wind (Boreas) while she was playing with her friend Pharmakeia (229c-d). It does not seem too much of a stretch to see the myth as pointing to the dual nature of Pharmakeia and to the potential danger of the area around the Nymphs' grove. Within the grove itself, the cicadas who sing in the plane-tree overhead represent a similar ambiguity. For those of weak mind these singers are like the Sirens in the *Odyssey*, casting a spell of forgetfulness, bringing sleep, but if human beings can sail past their bewitchment and keep on talking, the cicadas will give them a gift of honor, reporting to the Muses in heaven the nature of each person. Those who have gone through life loving wisdom and honoring the musical arts of the highest Muses Kalliope (Beautiful Voice) and Ourania (Heavenly), will be especially honored as the cicadas (see above) will announce their achievements to those two Muses (258e-259d).

At the end of the dialogue, the question is raised whether writing is a *pharmakon* for memory (i.e., a medicine against forgetting or a poison aiding forgetting); also see *Cicadas*.

Eros (Love), friend (*philos*), friendship (*philotes* and *philia*)

In Hesiod's *Theogony*, limb-loosening (*lysimelos*) Eros is the third god to emerge out of Chaos, after Earth and Tartara. He is both an anthropomorphic figure and the personification of a primordial and cosmic generating force, familiar to modern readers from Freud's principles of Eros and Thanatos (Love and Death). In the *Theogony* he attends Aphrodite's birth and thereafter in Greek literature appears frequently in her company. In the sixth century, one poet makes him the offspring of Aphrodite and Ares, although many variants circulate. In Sappho, for example, he is the son of Ouranos and Gaia (or Aphrodite). Anacreon is the first to describe his nature as the playful tempter and Euripides is the first to associate him with the bow and arrow. In Plato's *Symposium*, Phaedrus, following Hesiod, says that he is among the oldest of the gods, while Agathon says that he is the most fair and beautiful of the gods, and the youngest. Socrates in the *Symposium* says that he is the son of Wealth and Poverty, an in-between figure always searching for fulfillment. In the *Republic*, he is called a tyrant (9.573b). The associations of *eros* as lower case noun do not differ greatly from those of the god: a sexual force, which the Greeks viewed as a disease that assaults the body and makes the mind go mad.

The adjective *philos* means "dear" or "beloved" and as a substantive noun means "friend." It often appears in the dialogue as a form of address, as it does in the opening sentence when Socrates addresses "my dear Phaedrus." On one occasion Socrates addresses Phaedrus by the noun *philotes*, "my friendship," or "my love" (228d), a form of address found in

Aristophanes. Often the distinction in meaning between *philotes* and *philia* is slight, both referring to "friendship," "affection," but the older word (*philotes*), especially in Homer and Hesiod, can commonly also refer to "sexual intercourse." At 255e, the beloved is said to mistake *eros* for *philia*. Philosophy literally refers to someone who is a friend or lover of *sophia* ("wisdom"). See also *Lover* and *Beloved, To Love*, and *Vocative addresses*.

Mortals call the god "winged Eros," but the gods simply say "Winged," most likely for the same reason that mortals depict an erect penis as a winged bird. See Appendix C.

Fable (*mythos*)

Fable (or our myth) translates the marked word for story (*logos* being the unmarked word). In Plato, Socrates often criticizes fable for its falsehoods and imperfect representations of true Being, but he frequently resorts to fable and myth-making himself to advance philosophy. These fables most commonly accentuate a point within a philosophic discussion by describing something which dialectic cannot reach. Major portions of a dialogue may be a *mythos*, as for example Books II-XI of the *Republic* describing the City in Speech (2.378c and 382d). Some scholars believe that Socrates resorts to myth as a convenience when talking with those who have not yet seen the truth, but that condition befalls the teacher himself as Socrates more than once reminds any who listen.

When calling on the Muses at the beginning of his first speech, he describes his narration as a fable (237a), and he will again refer to that speech as a fable after he has delivered his speech (241e; cf. 243a). From the start, he delivered that speech in shame and one might say that the word fable is used pejoratively to describe it. But one must realize that the story of the charioteer in the palinode is no less a fable (253c). Unlike the fable of the first speech, this one is in the service of the gods and, by describing realms of truth which are beyond the reach of philosophic dialectic, this fable will set the stage, however obliquely, for the philosophical discussion of the art of rhetoric which follows it.

Socrates also describes the hymn to Love as mythic (265c). According to Phaedrus, Socrates is "mythologizing" when he talks about justice and such things (276e).

Form(s) (*eidos, eidea*)

There is nothing for which Plato is more famous than his theory of Forms, perhaps most succinctly articulated in Socrates' discussion of the Divide Line in the *Republic* (VI.509d-511e). Forms are part of the invisible realm of Being, as distinct from the physical, mortal realm of Becoming. Although the forms by definition cannot be seen with the senses, Socrates describes them, for the benefit of mortals, in visual terms, as when he says that souls on the rim of heaven "gaze on things outside the heavens" (247c). He also describes them in the language of initiation (cf. 250c and note 76) (see *Initiation*). For a definition of a Form, or at least for a description of what it is (from a human perspective), see Socrates at 249b in the palinode: "that which, going from a plurality of perceptions is drawn together by reasoning into a single essence." The Form is a singularity, or the thing itself, of what on earth looks like a plurality; i.e., for the many chairs of this earth there is a single, invisible form Chair from which the many on earth derive.

The word for invisible forms also describes the "forms" of speech (265a). As the subsequent discussion of rhetoric shows, this is not a causal use of the term. Understanding the forms of the universe and the forms of speech both involve a similar ability to navigate back and forth between the one and the many and to discover an underlying unity in plurality. Also see *Dialectic*.

Friend, Friendship, see Eros.

Grove (place) (*ho topos*), or **resting place** (*katagoge*)

The word for "resting place" (*katagoge*, 230b) more literally means "bringing down." The motion downward also makes possible upward lift, and the grove is equally a place of ascent, as is suggested by the "lofty" (230b) plane tree and the cicadas who carry word back to the heavenly Muses.

Almost every word used to describe the physical characteristics of the grove reappears later in the *Phaedrus* to reveal essential qualities about either love or rhetoric. For example, the many beauties (*pankalos*; 230b4, c4) of the scene may anticipate the celebration of beauty which enters the earthbound soul through the eyes and stirs her to recollect heavenly Beauty seen by the mind's eye alone (cf. 249d-252c). In the discussion of rhetoric, Phaedrus praises Socrates for speaking "absolutely beautifully" (*pankalos*) about things "most beautiful" (*kallista*) (274a; cf. 276e; at 269a and 271c *pankalos* is clearly ironic).

Socrates describes the breeze which blows through the grove as *metrios* (see below), a word which most naturally would be translated here as "moderate" (229b) if it weren't for the fact that *metrios* runs like a neural pathway through the whole dialogue describing the quality of Socrates' "measured" speech. This latter usage prompts me to translate the grove's *pneuma metroin* as a "well-measured breeze." This breeze is also described as "adorable," *agapeton* (230c), from the verb *agapeo* (see above), one of the three verbs used in the *Phaedrus* to describe love. Only in the most uncommon of circumstances does this verb convey sexual intercourse; more typically it describes the kind of love that a father has for a son. But Socrates' wrong-headed first speech ends with a striking use of the verb: a lover's friendship is a hunger, he says; "as wolves adore (*agaposin*) lambs, so lovers (*erastai*) are fond of (*philousin*) boys" (241d). In the palinode, this adoration describes more fittingly what lovers feel when looking upon eternal Being (cf. 247d).

Also relevant in this context is the "perfectly gracious spring" (*pege khariestate*) that flows (*rhei*) under the plane tree in the grove. In a daringly imagined portrait, desire is figured as a spring (*pege*) that "flows upon the lover—a spring from the stream which Zeus, loving Ganymede, called Himeros (Desire), the waters of desire entering into the lover and overflowing around the boy once the lover has become saturated" (255bc). In Socrates' bold etymology of the word Himeros, he imagines the word coming from "portions" (*mere*) and "flowing" (*rheonta*): the soul of the lover warmed and refreshed as the soul takes in deep draughts (portions) of the boy's in-flowing beauty (251c). In all cases, a quality of the grove's physical characteristics appears to provide a physical and linguistic preparation for central visionary and philosophical themes which take place within the grove.

The *locus amoenus* of pastoral poetry, where poets in the simplicity and leisure of a country setting under the shade of a tree, sing and compete with songs (often about love), owes much to Plato's description of this grove. For these comparisons, as well as for references to groves as centers of worship for the shepherds and other members of the humbler Athenian classes, see Gutzwiller (1991). In reference to the plane tree (*platanos*), one wonders whether Plato (*Platon* in the nominative, *Platonos* in the gentive) isn't punning on his own name (as perhaps also at 246c7).

Hybris (*hybristikos*)

Aristotle defines hybris: "Doing and saying things at which the victim incurs shame in order…simply to get pleasure from it" (*Rhetoric* 1378b). *Hybris* ranges in meaning from "wanton violence" including rape, arising from pride of might or passion, to "lust," to "insolence" or "arrogance." It always violates a general Greek sense of moral or social order, and is often punished therefore by the gods, if not by men. The noun appears twice in Lysias' speech at 238a where it is translated "excess." It also appears six times in Socrates' palinode: at 250e (noun) where it is translated as "wantonness" to describe sexual desire; and at 253e (noun), 254c (adjective), and 254e (twice: once noun, once adjective) where it is translated again as "wanton" or "wanton excess" to describe the black horse. At 252b it describes the Homeric verse on god-talk about Eros where it is translated "utterly outrageous."

In due measure, in measure, see *Unskilled speaker*.

In prose, in verse, see *Unskilled speaker*.

Initiation (*telete, telestikos, telesterion*)

Initiation into the mysteries is the second of the four forms of divine madness; through prayer and purification rites which are associated with the god Dionysos (cf. 265b), mortals can find deliverance from sickness and toils, particularly in regard to sicknesses and toils which pass down like an inheritance in certain families (cf. 244e-245a). But when it comes to ranking souls which have the keenest sight of the hyperouranian vision (i.e., of the forms; cf. 247b-c), the initiated soul is ranked a lowly fifth out of a field of nine (cf. 248e).

But in a more positive passage, Socrates associates the soul's *recollection* of heavenly beauty and her proper handling of the *reminders* of the *forms* with initiation (cf. 250b-c). In one passage, Socrates plays extensively on the root *tele-* found both in terms for initiation and for perfection or completeness. His play of terms almost defies translation: *teleous aei teletas teloumenos, teleos ontos*, 249c. The adjective *teleos* describes something which is perfect, complete, and without blemish; the noun *teletai* refers to initiations in the mystery rites, while *teloumenos* means both "being initiated" and "being made complete or made perfect." I render: only a man "who is perpetually initiated into these perfect mysteries is truly perfect." No person or soul, of course, is capable of such perfection, or of looking perpetually on the sight of Being (cf. 248b). Plato's imagery of initiation and perfection draws on Orphic terminology, as he does his reference to 1,000 and 10,000 year cycles, each of which represents an Orphic period. See Hackforth's commentary (pp. 82-4) and Linforth; also see *Recollection* and *Form*.

The language for perfection also describes rhetoric. A speaker must combine knowledge, practice, and natural ability to be "complete" or "perfect" (269c-d), Pericles being the "most perfect of all" (269e), language assuredly tinged with irony. But at 276b, a farmer who employs his art seriously can plant things which will reach "perfection," an analogy designed to help us understand how "writing in the soul" about things just, beautiful and good can be "clear, perfect, and worthy of seriousness" (278a). Such writing can serve as "reminders for men who know" (278a). This is not the language of initiation but it does echo the language of 249c where initiation is explicit. Unlike the vision of Being described in the palinode, there is no need for divine possession to reach perfection in the art of rhetoric. Also see *Divine Possession*.

To Love (*eraomai*), **to be fond of** (*phileo*), **to adore** (*agapao*)

Of the three verbs for love in the dialogue, *eraomai* always refers to sexual attraction or activity, as do the nouns related to it: *eros* ("love"), *erastes* ("lover"), *eromenos* ("beloved"). *Phileo*, related to *philos* ("dear" or "friend") usually refers to love in the sense of befriending, but as in English befriending can lead to something more physical. In five instances in this dialogue, it refers to a friendly affection and I translate "to be fond of," but at 231c it describes the affections which a lover feels for a beloved and at 253c the feelings of a beloved for a lover, and twice it refers to kissing (255e and 256a, and see note 88). *Agapao* frequently describes familial love as between a father and son; it rarely has sexual connotations. In the translation of the Hebrew Bible into Greek (the *Septuagint*) and then in the Christian Bible, the verb describes the love of God for man and vice versa. It appears six times in the dialogue and I always translate it "to adore." In one instance in the *Phaedrus*, Socrates uses the verb provocatively to describe a beast's predatory adoration of its prey, where a physical desire is unmistakable; the use of *phileo* is also striking in this phrase: "as wolves *adore* lambs, so *lovers* (*erastai*) *are fond of* a boy" (241d) (see note 53 in the translation). The sentence is clearly designed to seize attention: it concludes Socrates' first speech; the last half of it is in dactylic meter; the verbs are deliberately meant to surprise. Socrates uses an adjective from the verb *agapao* to describe the adorable breeze which flows through the grove (230c), one of many instances where a word describing the physical characteristics of the grove will take on a wider and more complex meaning later in the dialogue.

Lover (*erastes*), **beloved** (*eromenos*), **boy** (*pais*), **darling** (*paidika*)

The relation between lover and beloved is described in the Introduction (p. xi) and the Interpretative Essay (pages 74-5).

Maker of speeches, see *Unskilled speaker*.

Mind, see *Thinking*.

Memory, see *Recollection*.

Moderation (*sophrosyne*), **mortal moderation** (*sophrosyne thnete*)

Literally sound mind or thinking, moderation is the virtue common to the three parts of the soul and the three classes of citizens in the *Republic*. In line with other works by Plato, moderation in the *Phaedrus* is associated with reason and restraint in opposition to appetite and desire (241a). In the palinode, furthermore, it is honored along with justice and knowledge (250b and 247d), on a pedestal with heavenly beauty (254b), and it is listed among the laudatory qualities of the white horse (253d). But in the palinode Socrates also chastises this highest of Platonic virtues as he does in no other Platonic dialogue, condemning mortal moderation for its miserly, economizing, and slavish nature, saying that alone, without mad love, it will prevent a soul from sprouting wings and witnessing heavenly Beauty (256e; cf. 244d and 256b).

Necessity, see *Plausibility*.

Pharmakeia, see *Drug*.

Plausibility (*eikos*), **necessity** (*ananke*)

Eikos is the neuter participle of *eoika* "to be like," the third person singular *eoike* used commonly as an impersonal verb to mean "it is likely, reasonable, befitting." Words for probability, likelihood, or plausibility, that is, the participle *eikos* (in the singular) and *eikota* (in the plural), are hallmarks of sophistic rhetoric. The most famous proponent of advancing a case by arguments of plausibility rather than by factual evidence or informed knowledge of a subject is reported to be Tisias from Syracuse (cf. 267a-b), perhaps a student of Corax (see the Translation note 136) and himself a fifth-century rhetorician who was probably dead by the time the dialogue was supposed to take place (see the Translation note 123). Socrates addresses Tisias directly in his climactic comments about rhetoric, arguing that a true rhetorician must first have a philosophic understanding of the truth about a wide range of subjects (272e-274a; cf. 259e-260e).

In his speech Lysias repeatedly relies upon this technique, explicitly making an argument of probability four times (see note 21). The argument in Socrates' first speech, by contrast, is predicated upon necessity, a term he applies equally to the necessary ways an argument should be made and to the passions which follow rules of inevitability in their power over reason (see the Translation note 42).

The adverbial form *eikotos* and the adjectival form *eikos* are often translated as "likely" or "in all likelihood."

Poet, see *Unskilled speaker*.

Recollection (*anamnesis*), **a reminder** (*hypomnena*), **a reminding** (*hypomnesis*), **memory** (*mnene*)

Hesiod in the *Theogony* (233-36) implies that truth (*a-letheia*) is the negation of forgetting (*lethe*). Truth is the un-forgotten. In the heavens, as Socrates imagines in the palinode, souls contemplate the truth directly and look upon the Being which really is (cf. 247 c-e). But even in heaven, souls eventually become burdened with forgetfulness and wrongdoing and cannot see the truth (cf. 248c-e). At such times, they lose their wings and fall to earth. Only a soul which has seen the truth can enter into a human body (cf. 249b). Through a process of "recall" or "recollection," *anamnesis*, literally a "remembering back" or "remembering again," the "discursive thinking" of philosophers retains memory of these former times. Only the soul of someone who "correctly handles such *reminders (hypomnenata)* and is perpetually initiated into these perfect mysteries is truly perfect" (249c). Through love, the souls of divinely-possessed lovers can also regain memory of these distant things (250a-251a). It is too much for mortals to be wise; that is a blessing reserved for the gods, but a human can be a lover of wisdom (278d) and he can "reach for the beautiful" (274a-b), In the *Republic* this is achieved through a combination of dialectic and love of learning.

In the story of the invention of writing, the Egyptian god-king Ammon makes a sharp distinction between extemporaneous speech and writing, the latter being characterized as a system for reminding and thereafter as an aid ultimately for forgetting (274e-275b and 277e-2788a), but in the palinode Socrates offers a more nuanced inter-relation between recollection and reminders (cf. 249c) and writing in the soul . See Interpretative Essay, pages 97-9. See also *Initiation, Form. Thinking,* and *Arrangement.*

Reminder, reminding, see *Recollection.*

Resting place, see *Grove.*

Skill, see *Art.*

Skilled craftsman, see *Unskilled speaker.*

Speeches, see *Drug.*

Speech-maker, see *Unskilled speaker.*

Thinking, thought, mind, discursive thinking *(dianoia),* **thought** *(phronesis)*

Dianoia is among the most difficult words to translate in the *Phaedrus.* At 244c, Socrates gives an etymology of the word as if it consisted of a merging of *dia-* "through" or "thoroughly," *nous* "mind," and *historia* "inquiry." In most contexts, I translate it as "thinking" (228d), "thought" (234c, 244c, 265e, 270a), or "mind" (239a, 239c, 256c, 259a), but when referring to divine thought (247d), the philosopher (249c), the soul (256a), and the true rhetoricians (259e) I translate it as "discursive thinking." *Phronesis* is a common word in much of Plato but appears only once in this dialogue (250d).

Unskilled speaker *(idiotes),* **skilled craftsman, speech-maker, maker of speeches, poet** *(poietes),* **in due measure** (OR) **in verse** *(en metro),* **without measure** (OR) **in prose** *(aneu metrou),* **in measured speech** *(metrios)*

Plato uses a constellation of three words; *idiotes, poietes, metrios* with great wit and playfulness throughout the dialogue, in ways that have gone unnoticed. By the end of the dialogue, we see Socrates invoke, and then subsume, the conventional distinctions between written and extemporaneous speech and between poetry and prose. As in the *Symposium* where the philosopher absorbs and transforms the cultural divide between tragedy and comedy, so in this dialogue he absorbs contrasting views about rhetoric and transforms them into a philosophic synthesis. On the one hand, Socrates' speech-making is extemporaneous, and thus it is capable of being "ensouled" and "alive." Such speech is necessary for philosophy and the turning of souls. The word he uses for himself as an extemporaneous speaker is *idiotes*. On the other, his speech is crafted and measured (*metrios*) in the manner of those who write their speeches. The term for such a speech-writer is *poietes*; it is also the term for a poet who is divinely possessed while speaking. See the Interpretative Essay, pages 91-4.

The primary meaning of *idiotes* is political, referring to a person who is not engaged in the affairs of the *polis*; as a secondary meaning, it refers to a person who is unskilled and is sometimes translated as amateur. In its primary sense *idiotes* stands in opposition to *polites*, an engaged citizen, a word which does not appear in this dialogue (not surprisingly as the dialogue takes Socrates outside the city), but in the *Phaedrus* it stands in opposition to *poietes*.

It is an opposition which Socrates makes about himself. When he decides to challenge Lysias, he questions how he, an *idiotes*, improvising on the spot, can go up against a fine *poietes*: <u>agathon</u> poieten idiotes <u>autoschediazon</u> (236d; cf. 234e) As we see in this four word cluster, the nouns *poietes* and *idiotes* are in the middle facing off one against the other, flanked on either side by their adjectives, "good" vs. "extemporizing." Elsewhere in Plato *autoschediazo* has a pejorative meaning, referring to ill-advised thought or speech; cf. *Apology* 20d1, *Euthyphro* 5a7, 16a2. In Socrates' distinction between *poietes* and *idiotes*, he appears to use extemporizing once again in a pejorative sense, distinguishing crafted, prepared written texts from unskilled speeches made up on the spot. Phaedrus used *idiotes* with precisely the same connotation earlier in the dialogue (228a). Both Socrates and Phaedrus would lead one to believe that an *idiotes* would have no chance against a *poietes*. In this challenge between writers of speeches and extemporaneous speakers Socrates is echoing a current debate among Athenian rhetoricians: *poietes logon*, "a maker of words (or speeches)," comes close to being a technical term for a careful (prose) writer of speeches (see Isocrates 15.192 and Alkidamas' "On the writers of written speeches" 34, quoted in Appendix D). Since Socrates also uses the more neutral term for prose writer, *syngrapheus* (235c, 235e, 258a, 272b, 278e) throughout the *Phaedrus*, one must believe that when he uses the term *poietes* he does so for special effect. Indeed, his use of *poietes* is particularly playful and the cause of endless difficulties for translators.

At times, the word seems to offer little ambiguity. The first occurrences of *poietes* in the *Phaedrus* clearly refer to a skilled prose writer (at 234e and 236d); later references to poet are equally clear (at 245a, 247c, and 278e). But at other times Socrates teases our expectations, as in the phrase *ek tou theatrou ho poietes* (258b). At first glance, with theater preceding *poietes*, the phrase seems straightforward: "a poet [leaving] the theater," but Socrates is clearly talking about prose writers and *ho poietes* must be understood as a shorthand for *poietes logon,* and translated "a maker of speeches [leaving] the theater." See the Interpretative Essay, page 92 and note 98.

Twenty-five lines later Socrates continues the play. As in the previous example, the phrase seems clear enough until the last word: *en metro hos poietes e aneu metrou hos idiotes*: "in meter as a poet or without meter as an *idiotes* (258d). The Greek dictionary will tell you that *idiotes* here means "prose writer," although the dictionary gives no other reference for the word carrying this meaning and at 228a and 236d *idiotes* implicitly refers to a *non*-writer. Furthermore, the context is unmistakably about prose writers, making this sudden shift to poets and meter abrupt.

Once we get to the end of the phrase, we must go back and reinterpret it; reinterpretation turns on the word *metron*, which in its root meaning is translated as "measure," and by context can be translated as verse. So here, it initially seems to mean verse until the last word in the sentence. For various efforts at translation, see Interpretative Essay, page 40 and note 100. While it is possible to translate the last phrase "without verse as an unskilled speaker," I wonder whether the primary meaning of *metron* does not also hold here. Throughout the dialogue, and especially near the end of it, Socrates is said to speak *metrios*, the adverbial form of *metron* with translation ranging from (1) "moderately" or "in due measure," (2) "enough," to (3) "modestly, temperately." The paradoxical quality of Socrates' speech is that although he is an *idiotes* and by definition speaks *aneu metrou*, he also speaks *metrios* (236a, 265c, 277b, 278b, 279c) and *poietes*-like. With the life and soul of living speech, Socrates's language is also smartly crafted by years of dialectical training and discipline (271a-272b and 273d-274a), and he, as a true lover, is open to divinely inspired (poetic) language. With these complexities in mind, the passage here seems to be playing with expectation and with conventional boundaries of differentiation to highlight through verbal play the unique qualities of Socratic speech. Also see *Art* and *Grove*.

Vocative addresses

Socrates calls Phaedrus friend (*phile*) (11X), companion (*hetaire*) (7X), excellent fellow (*ariste*) (3X), my good man (*agathe*) (3X), brave (*pheriste*) (2X), blessed (*makarie*) (2X), divinely inspired (*daimonie*) (2X), young man (*neania*) (1X), darling boy (*pai*)(1X), love (or friend) (*philotes*) (1X), brute (*miare*) (1X). Socrates also says that Phaedrus is a dear head (translated as dear heart) and most dear (*philtatos*). Further, Socrates puns on Phaedrus' name in the play between Phaedrus and *paid'* at 261a (and again at 265c). The same play seems active at the end of Socrates' first speech with *hos paida*, describing a lover loving "the darling," quickly followed by *o Phaidre*, "this is the speech, my Phaedrus" (241d). And Socrates puns on Phaedrus' name which means "bright," linking bright Phaedrus through puns with Ganymede, "Bright Counsels," Zeus' darling and Phaedrus' mythic counterpart in the palinode (234d and 255c). Without question, Phaedrus, the bright and beautiful "boy," stirs Socrates with desire. By contrast, Phaedrus rarely addresses Socrates by anything other than his name, but he twice calls him *phile*, reciprocating Socrates' address. He also calls "my astonishing man" (*thaumasie*) (2x), "my most noble man" (*gennaiotate* (1X), and "my best man" (*beltiste*) (1X). The different quality in the nature of these addresses echoes what we might imagine to be the difference in the way a lover and beloved addressed one another.

Without measure, see *Unskilled speaker*.

Writing, see *Drug*.

SELECTED BIBLIOGRAPHY

TEXTS AND COMMENTARIES

Brisson, Luc (ed. & tr.). 1989. *Platon: "Phèdre"* (Paris), with Jacques Derrida, *La Pharmacie de Platon* (1972)

Burnet, John (ed.). 1903. *Platonis Opera* vol. II (Oxford))

Reale, Giovanni (ed., tr,, and notes). 1998. *Platone Fedro* (Lorenzo Valla)

Verdenius, W. J. 1955. "Notes on Plato's *Phaedrus*," *Mnemosyne* 8, 265-89

de Vries, G. J. 1969. *A Commentary on the Phaedrus of Plato* (Amsterdam)

TRANSLATIONS

Cobb, William (tr.). 1993. *The Symposium and the Phaedrus: Plato's Erotic Dialogues* (Albany)

Hackforth, R. (tr.). 1952. *Plato's Phaedrus* (Cambridge)

Nehamas, Alexander and Woodruff, Paul (tr.). 1995. *Phaedrus.* (Indianopolis)

Nichols, James (tr.). 1998. *Plato. Phaedrus* (Ithaca)

Rowe, C. J. (ed. & tr.). 1986. *Plato: Phaedrus* (Warminster)

BIBLIOGRAPHY

Lustrum 4 (1959), 5 (1960), 20 (1977), 25 (1983), 30 (1988), 34 (1992)

SECONDARY CRITICISM

Allen, Michael (ed. & tr.). 1981. *Marsilio Ficino and the Phaedrean Charioteer* (Berkeley)

——. 1984. *The Platonism of Marsilio Ficino* (Berkeley)

Asmis, Elizabeth. 1986. "*Psychagogia* in Plato's *Phaedrus*," *Illinois Classical Studies* 11, 153-72

Benardete, Seth. 1991. *The Rhetoric of Morality and Philosophy: Plato's Gorgias and Phaedrus* (Chicago)

Burger, Ronna. 1980. *Plato's Phaedrus: A Defense of a Philosophic Art of Writing* (Birmingham)

Cole, Thomas. 1991. *The Origins of Rhetoric in Ancient Greece* (Baltimore)

Demos, Marian. 1999. *Lyric Quotation in Plato* (Lanham, Maryland)

Ferrari, G. R. F. 1987. *Listening to the Cicadas. A Study of Plato's Phaedrus* (Cambridge)

Foley, Helene. 1988. "'The Mother of the Argument:' Eros and the Body in Sappho and Plato's *Phaedrus*," in M. Wyke (ed.) *Parchments of Gender* (Oxford) 39-70

Friedländer, Paul. 1958. *Plato* vol. I: *An Introduction* (tr. Hans Meyerhoff) (New York)

Griswold, Charles. 1986. *Self-Knowledge in Plato's Phaedrus* (New Haven)

——. 2002. "Irony in the Platonic Dialogues," *Philosophy and Literature* 26, 84-106

Gutzwiller, Kathryn. 1991. *Theocritus' Pastoral Analogies* (Madison)

Heath, Malcolm. 1989. "The Unity of Plato's *Phaedrus*," *Oxford Studies in Ancient Philosophy* 7, 151-73 and 189-91

Hubbard, T. K. (ed.) 2003. *Homosexuality in Greece and Rome: A Sourcebook of Basic Documents* (Berkeley)

Janaway, Christopher. 1995. *Images of Excellence: Plato's Critique of the Arts* (Oxford)

Lebeck, Anne. 1972. "The Central Myth of Plato's *Phaedrus*," *GRBS* 13, 267-90

Linforth, , I. M. 1946. "The Corybantic Rites in Plato" and "Telestic Madness in Plato's *Phaedrus* 244DE," *University of California Proceedings in Classical Philology* 13, 121-62 and 163-82, respectively.

Nicholson, Graeme. 1999. *Plato's Phaedrus: The Philosophy of Love* (W. Lafayette, Indiana)

Nightingale, Andrea. 1995. *Genres in Dialogues. Plato and the Construct of Philosophy* (Cambridge)

Nietzsche, Friedrich. 1924. "The Problem of Socrates" *Twilight of the Idols* in *Fall Wagner* (tr. Thomas Common) (New York)

Nussbaum, Martha. 1986. *The Fragility of Goodness. Luck and Ethics in Greek Tragedy and Philosophy* (Cambridge)

Roochnik, David. 1996. *Of Art and Wisdom: Plato's Understanding of Techne* (University Park)

Rosen, Stanley. 1993. *The Quarrel between Philosophy and Poetry* (New York)

Rossetti, L. (ed.) 1992. *Understanding the Phaedrus* (Sankt Augustin)

Rowe, C. J. 1989. "The Unity of the *Phaedrus*: A Reply to Heath," *Oxford Studies in Ancient Philosophy* 7, 175-88

Rutherford, R. B. 1995. *The Art of Plato* (Cambridge, Mass.)

Schloemann, Johan. 2002. "Entertainment and Democratic District: The Audience's Attitude towards Oral and Written Oratory in Classical Athens," in Ian Worthington and John Miles Foley (eds.) *Epea and Grammata: Oral and Written Communication in Ancient Greece*, Mnemosyne Suppl. 230 (Leiden) 133-46

de Vries, G. J. 1971. "Isocrates in the *Phaedrus*: A Reply," *Mnemosyne* 24, 387-90

White, David. 1993. *Rhetoric and Reality in Plato's Phaedrus* (Albany)

Yunis, Harvey. 1996. *Taming Democracy: Models of Political Rhetoric in Classical Athens* (Ithaca) 172-210